GETTING INSIDE OUT

Simon N Cooper

Copyright © 2005 Simon N Cooper

Reprinted 2007

First published by
Slice Innovations (Publishing)
76 Tudor Way, Worcester WR2 5QU
www.sliceinnovations.co.uk
Registered in England and Wales No. 5771116

The right of Simon N Cooper to be identified as the Author of this work has been asserted to him in accordance with the Copyright, Designs and Patents Act 1988.

All Rights reserved.
No part of this publication may be reproduced, stored in a retrieval system or transmitted in any form or by any means, electronic, mechanical, photocopying, recording, or otherwise, without the prior permission of the publisher or a license permitted restricted copying. In the UK, such licenses are issued by the Copyright Licensing Agency, 90 Tottenham Court Road, London W1P 9HE

British Library Cataloguing in Publication Data
A catalogue record for this book is available from the British Library

ISBN 0-9557150-0-6

All Bible References have been based upon the New Life Good News Bible first published 1976

Cover design & Typeset by Slice Design

GETTING INSIDE OUT

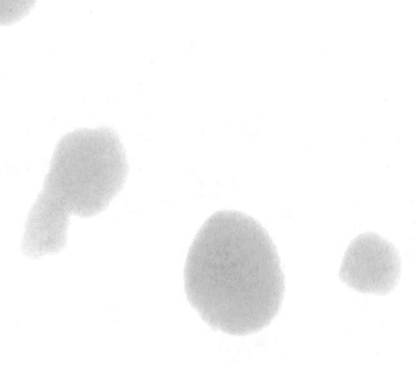

Dedicated to my wife, Laura, who puts up with all my crazy ideas and schemes, yet still supports me all the same

CONTENTS

GET IN

Identity Check	15
Back in my day...	18
Losing my religion	21
Mirror Image	27
Night-Vision	30
Rocking & Rolling	36

GO OUT

Be Wise	43
Onions	47
Blessya	51

HEAVEN-SENT

Riding the Waves	61
Barking Up the Right Tree	68
Accepting Grace	74

EASTER PROMISE

Taking it too far	81
Number One	85
Seeing is Believing	91
Prove It!	93

BACK TO BASICS

Rich Tea & Baptistery	**103**
House Fire	**111**
Take a Deep Breath	**113**

CHANGING YOUR ANGLE

You can't please everyone, can you?	**119**
Love is...	**124**
Child Prophecy	**126**

GET INTO GEAR

Do as I say!	**135**
Excuse me!	**138**

LET US PRAY

Reading the Script	**149**

FOREWORD
By Rev J Neil Adams

I have had the privilege of getting to know Simon first as a member of my Church and latterly as a friend.

I first met Simon when I became his minister in the Methodist Church in Hinckley in Leicestershire, where he was running our Youth Fellowship. It has been great to see him grow and answer a call I saw clearly in him to preach. He leads worship with a clear passion for Jesus and under the anointing of the Holy Spirit.

Si & I have become friends over these last five years and I had the honour of presiding at his marriage to Laura in 2006.

He is a good Christian young man who will no doubt be used mightily by God.

INTRODUCTION

Being a young child, I used to sleep under a very snug quilt adorned in the image of Spiderman, my favourite superhero. Able to shoot webs from his wrists and defend against evil, he' a legend the world over, with movies still being made about him! However, like many superheroes, Spiderman is an alter-ego – one of humble Peter Parker, a photographer selling pictures to the local paper.

Maybe, just maybe, Christians have managed to acquire the art of keeping everything inside – good at portraying our own desired, heroic alter-ego to our churches, whilst being something completely different inside! God knows what we desire and exactly what goes on inside yet He is still totally crazy about us. We don't need to have alter-egos - instead, we can try hard to get what's inside out of us. After all, do friends really know all the desires of our hearts? I hope that through this book, you'll find out what's going on inside of me and some of the desires of my heart.

Through a collection of thoughts, readings, poems, drama and prayers, I hope that in some way, they will inspire and challenge you. On the other hand, you could just see them as one man nattering away! If that is the case, I hope you enjoy my nattering as I try and get my inside out of me.

Simon N Cooper

GET IN
Finding out what is on the inside

IDENTITY CHECK

It's a really difficult question to answer sometimes. What makes me tick? What is my identity? Where have I been in life? How did I get here? Who am I?

I think that in everyone's life, there comes a time when we do look inside and try to really find out just what we're about. Sometimes we don't like it but it is important to know our identity.

I studied for a course once and had to complete a personal profile. Where did my focus lie? It was like a professional version of those completely meaningless, but very tempting questionnaires that you get posted through the door, desperate to know what washing-up liquid you buy and where you go on your holidays. I have to admit that I've enjoyed filling some of those in. However, I had to really think about what it was that made 'me'. I have to say that it revealed a few surprises.

We all have lots of different shapes to our lives and these make us who we are. As well as being an idiot and a non-stop jabberer, I find that I have various identities. I'm a husband, a son and a grandson. I'm a Brit, from the Midlands and I could even say that I'm a Worcester-farian. I'm a Hinckley United fan, a U2 fan, and I'm partial to mushrooms. But with all of them, I'm still Simon Cooper.

Jesus had lots of ways of describing himself and we understand him more from these. Here are some ways from a children's service of looking at who he said he was.

IDENTITY CHECK

Jesus said: "I am the bread!"

Bread is nice, it makes us full, it feeds us every day.
Jesus fed 5000 men, in a very special way.
Now we need bread, to help us live, we need Jesus as well
So let Him be a part of you, He's great to show and tell

Jesus said: "I am the light!"

We have light, it helps us see, it gets rid of the dark
A blind man by the poolside, where Jesus left his mark
He made him see, He gave him light, He gave him back his sight
The blackness ain't so scary, when Jesus is our light.

Jesus said: "I am the way!"

Signs help us; they direct us the way we want to go
Then we reach the place we want, whether high or whether low
Jesus rides right by our side; He guides us with His map
Clapping us along the way, and cheering every lap

Jesus said: "I am the Good Shepherd"

Jesus cares for every sheep in his well-tended flock
Standing watching patiently from His almighty rock
Everyone is worth as much, He searches for the lost
He tends each sheep, through thick and thin, no matter what the cost

Jesus said: "I am the life!"

Jesus came back from the grave, three days after He died
Then told the world: "I'm here to stay; I have no need to hide
Follow me, I'm all these things, the fight with death is won
I am the Life, I'm back from death, I'm God's amazing son!"

BACK IN MY DAY

As someone once said, "Life is a Roller-coaster". We all have our ups and downs and it seems that when we are down, that's when we begin questioning.

Who? What? Which? Where? When? How? Why? Why? Why?

Why? That's the most common question when we find things that don't go our way. "Why did it have to rain today?" "Why did I forget to do the laundry?" "Why did you take his life?" "Why me?" "Why?"

When you become a Christian, it's the wider world that thinks everything becomes rosy for you. Christians are Happy Boppy People who are always smiling and thanking God for everything. Sorry, from my experience, that isn't always possible. We do have times of difficulty, we have to cry and suffer.

I love those churches that praise God in every mishap. "Praise God – I've twisted my ankle!" "God has blessed me with Chicken Pox!" "Thanks for the broken window in our living room – Hallelujah!" You have to admire their faith – nothing can go wrong! They have a great belief in the fact that everything happens for a reason. God wanted them to hobble, to be spotty or live in their draughty lounge. That's not me I'm afraid. When things aren't going my way, I question God, but boy, when I've been blessed, I'm praising and worshipping Him.

When we're down, it's then that we look around. We try and find an easy way out. We compare ourselves to others that don't seem to be struggling. We say that we don't want to be a Christian any more. We don't want to follow his life. It seemed so easy when we first believed and yet, it's so hard. "It was better in the olden days!"

Yes, we all do it. We all get nostalgic, but we don't need to.
The next poem sees someone who is looking back enviously,
but they get their answer.

✪✪✪✪✪

BACK IN MY DAY

Why I follow Jesus is something I do ask?
With every sigh that bellows, through every God-called task.
It must have been so easy when there wasn't any fun
No TV to distract them, no housework to be done.

They couldn't do the hoovering, they couldn't iron shirts
They wouldn't have to mow the lawn - do they know how much that hurts?
If I could get rid of all that, I'd have a lot more time
Then following my Jesus would be absolutely fine.

I'd sit back in an armchair, with Bible and music on
And enjoy reading from Psalms today, as seconds tick along
To get rid of the hassle that surrounds in every way
Would make me follow Jesus just like them of yesterday

Yes, following Lord Jesus must be an easy life
No panic, worry, pressure, devoid of all the strife
That's what I want from Jesus, that's what I need today
That must be what the Christians are like, living their holy way

Then Jesus speaks, His tone is rough, He says "you want to relax?"
"I don't need to know you then, your understanding lacks!"
"To follow me, it's vital true, but hassle-free it ain't"
"Trust me, there's not an hour goes by without Christian complaint."

"The world out there, it needs some folk whose faith is crystal clear."
"But folk that live alongside me without that mortal fear."
"They do not muse, they do not look on all the days of yore"
"They march on through, they live for me, they want me evermore."

Then Jesus went, I sat and thought and something came to mind.
This Christian life, it's not for past, it's not always sweet and kind.
And so I asked for Jesus back to help me as a friend.
And we fought the trials hand in hand, from that day til the end.

And remember that the Christian life is not a time of ease.
Don't curse God when things are tough, I'm begging you that please
A Christian's life ain't sickly sweet; it's a struggle through and through.
But remember that your Saviour, He's been there ahead of you.

LOSING MY RELIGION

When you begin to talk all about your faith and the exciting things that the church can do, you leave yourself very open to strange questions, comments and things that take you aback. I can remember trying to persuade a friend to come to a youth group event which was quite fun when he popped up with the question – "That's one of those religious things, ain't it?" I was quick to answer "Yes, but it's different, it's fun!" He just laughed.

We need to be wary of associating ourselves to religion – society has given religion a label. After all, we are used to seeing people being killed, being beaten up, communities divided in the name of religion. Wars, battles, over history, all because of religion! The world, understandably, has conjured up a negative response to religion – a barrier has been formed when we try to share faith – "You're the religious type!" No, I'm not!

If only we could concentrate on not being religious, but make sure we have a faith, one that we can be proud of – oh, how much we would stand out! Religion, in Jesus' time, was associated with the Pharisees – the 'do as I say, not as I do' sector. It's still very relevant today. Churches are made up of people who let their religion block their faith – more concerned with how church is done, rather than concentrating on getting to know Jesus better.

Don't call me religious – call me a Christian!

LOSING MY RELIGION

REM are a pop group with a bit of a bizarre way with words. Coming to life in the 1980's, one of their songs contained the words "I'm pushing an elephant down the stairs!" Another has the incredibly lyrically sound song with the repetitive line – "Yeah, yeah, yeah, yeah!" Must have taken them years to come up with lyrics like that! Genius! Still, they have had many hit singles, and are still going at the moment.

But one of their songs that used to catch my ear by them is one with the following lines:

"That's me in the corner, that's me in the spotlight, losing my religion."

When I was a bit younger, I used to hear those words and get a little bit annoyed – maybe because it looked a bit bad on Christianity, maybe because it mentioned religion in a song, maybe because it was a negative statement, but whatever it was, it irked me.

Still, I was driving from a fast-food restaurant once and we picked up a radio station – one that plays the best of the Eighties, Nineties and today, and in between Keane and Queen, very confusing if you weren't in the know, came this REM song. This time it got me and I empathised with the words.

Here's my confession to you and if it shocks you, then so be it!

"I'M LOSING MY RELIGION!"

The reasons for this are numerous and I'd like to share some of the reasons with you.

I remember once, being in a church, they had a huge pulpit. It was the centrepiece of the church, but to renovate the place, it was to be taken out to be replaced by a platform where you can do lots more, and everyone can see! Would you believe the outrage and the audacity – that pulpit has been part of the church for so many years and how dare they take it away? Well, as you can imagine, people made a fuss – I thought for one minute that there was going to be a "Save our Pulpit" campaign. There became a divide, sharp words, hatred, enemies made, all done because of a pulpit.

Now, I don't like to sit on the fence – too much of that and you get splinters in your posterior! That pulpit needed to go. It was as if to some people that the pulpit was the most important part of the church and not Jesus. That helped me to begin to lose my religion – I didn't care what was in the church as long as God was there.

Another example – I've been to places where people have commented on my lack of tie when I preached and the fact that I took my jacket off because I was warm during the service – people decided that was what affected them. It hurt me, because what I was wearing did not alter the way that I'd tried to interpret God's word and I believed that it had been inspired by God. But to some people, my clothing was important, maybe more important than worshipping God. Again, that helped me to lose my religion. If being religious is about being uncomfortable then I didn't want to be there. I wanted to be comfortable with getting to know God better.

I'll stop now as you'll get the wrong impression of me and I'll sound like a whiner, but the fact of the matter is that I'm well on the way to losing my religion and I'm pretty happy with that. I've even got into the habit of sitting in different seats at church, but I still hold on to some things that would make me still religious. I still like to do some things in certain ways – I like to sing particular songs, like to do things the way that I feel comfortable, use the same rough format – I think that still makes me religious.

What I need to get clear is that being religious isn't about the 'olden days' – it's very much an aspect of church in general. Churches where they seem to pick the same songs nearly every week are evident, even in the evangelical movement.

Churches that let their legalistic theories become the focus of the church and place barriers instead of love between persecuted sections of society are numerous. They all have religious theories and that takes away the focus for the whole church. We don't want to be a religious generation, do we? I certainly pray that we're not.

I think that at times, we cling on to our traditions and make that our religion. It's so evident in churches – what do we cling on to all the time? Our cliques that we have – how accessible are they for other people to get into them? Our seats – do you have your own space that if you couldn't sit there, it would make you uncomfortable? I hold my hands up to both of them and say that I'm guilty of both of them. But we, as Christians, love to cling on to things that maybe just aren't that important in our faith.

Jesus was very anti-religion and was against the Pharisees – those that were seen as religious men. When people wanted to follow Him, He was very strict and realistic in the way it was going to be. Jesus actually said, in Luke 9: "If you can't hate your family, and your own life, then you can't follow me."

I know it's in the Bible, but don't get out anti-depressants, or tell your other half that you hate them, because I'm not quite sure that is what Jesus meant. What He means there is for people to give up what they hold on to. Jesus didn't want his followers to be pre-occupied with something else, maybe football, TV or any other idols that life would give – he wanted them to be totally focused on following Him. Think for yourself – what things in your life could possibly get in the way of you following Jesus?

We do get hung up on some things. Sometimes, there are things that take our priority, things that become our focus - it's these things that dominate our life. How many times have you seen reports and seen the fact that numbers who attend church are dwindling? That less people are interested in coming to church? I don't believe that's what's important. Or maybe it's the lack of young people in a congregation?

Churches are worried that not enough young people go to church. I'm not even sure that's at the top of God's list.

The first church in Acts 1 and 2 is probably a prime example of what Jesus meant when he said "take up your cross". You see, when they began life as a church without Jesus, they sat around and were constantly concerned with how many people were there and who should be in charge. Then suddenly, everything changed. Pentecost came and God sent out the Holy Spirit to really show everyone what the aim of being a follower of Christ was all about. He gave them tongues to speak the word of Christ, and empowered them to be disciples.

I remember hearing someone speak and with a church of 300, you would think that they were mightily blessed. But in the leader's sermon, he spoke and said "I would rather have a church of 50 committed disciples than 300 church members." A phrase which echoes Jesus who would rather have a number of disciples committed to following him and willing to carry the cross, than have a great number of followers who were hanging on to other things, who had other distractions.

Is it just a message for those days? No, it's not! Even today, we are called to kneel before Him, give up things that we like and follow Christ. Sometimes, it's hard, but it's the choice that we all have to make.

The trouble is, even in church, we are hung up on things like numbers and young people. That makes us forget that our priority should be sharing the faith that's within, preaching the gospel and making sure that the others get a taste of what it is like to be a Christian. That should be our priority – to take the message of Jesus to the world.

I think church, though, is so concerned with legalism, music, the comfortable seating, the colours of the notice board, rather than the real issue of making sure people can be strengthened as Christians. I even remember a church meeting where the focal point has been the price of the coffee rather than the way that the church was going. That's a big concern!

So, what do we do to head in the right direction? As a church, we need to remember that we are not religious folk, we are Christian folk. We are in the church because we believe Jesus is our Saviour, our friend and our brother and want to worship Him. For what he did for us, we need to take up the cross and really follow Him. Give our lives to Him. Open our hearts and receive the Holy Spirit into our lives to really gain a strong faith. Then we can be confident of carrying our cross into the world as a strong witness to the love of God!

So, think of our own lives? Think of the things that make us religious. Think of the things that we hang on to. Do they obstruct our relationship with Jesus? Remember what being a Christian is all about. After all, Jesus said that there are two commandments that outdo any others and they should take precedence. In Matthew 22, he said: "Love God" and "Love your neighbour as you love yourselves!"

The Ten Commandments are not to be ignored, our morals aren't to be eradicated, but only when we are confident of doing the loving bit, then we can be wise to help others.

I encourage you, if you have God at the centre, then concentrate on loving Him, loving Jesus and loving your neighbours. To be a success as a church, to encourage more people to get to know him, we need to start losing our religion and gaining our faith.

So get out there, share your faith, and don't be known as someone who is religious, be known as a wide-eyed, sanctified, bona-fide Christian and proud of it!

MIRROR IMAGE

Egos need popping sometimes! People who are so good-looking annoy me if they act like they know they are! No, it's not because I'm ugly or because of any petty jealousy, it's just their inflated egos.

We know what we are like and how to love ourselves. Let's just not go overboard about it!

✪✪✪✪✪

MIRROR IMAGE

How often do you watch a bit of television and see all of those adverts for either hair gel or toothpaste? There's a person at the sink, apparently just got up, despite the fact that they are looking great already. They smile into the mirror in the bathroom as if to say "Mmm, I'm looking great!" I'm sure there are people around that stand there, winking at themselves in the mirror. You know the vain types that look into the mirror in the morning and go "Hey gorgeous!" They must really love themselves!

However, that's not me! I'm not a morning person. Over the years, I've grown very fond of my bed – I like it! It keeps me safe at night. There does come a time in the morning when I wake up, usually about half an hour before work begins. I get up and go to the bathroom. I try to have a wash without looking in the mirror. It's an art form. However, sometimes I catch a glimpse of myself and think "Urgh!" I can't stand that. It's the same with photos - I just don't like looking at them.

I don't think that's what Jesus really meant when he said we are to love our neighbour as we love ourselves. He didn't want us to go up to people and say "Wow, you are looking absolutely marvellous", "I love your hair!" That's not what He meant.

Now I'm not too hot on my appearance as are most people. I could lose a few pounds, I could look after my skin better, but that doesn't mean I don't love myself. I do love myself. So often, that phrase is taken the wrong way. You see people look at others and hear them say "Oh, yeah, Doris, he really loves himself!" Well, I say good! He should love himself.

You see, I do love myself and here's the reason why. Whenever I get hungry, I make sure I have food. Whenever I'm thirsty, I make sure I can have a drink. Whenever I get cold, I make sure I can find some way of getting warm. Whenever I have ragged clothes, I make sure I get some new ones. Whenever it gets wet, I make sure I have shelter. Whenever I need rest, I sleep in a comfortable place. I look after myself. I make sure that I am safe and well.

I need to do all this. For a simple reason – to live! You see, God has made me. He has entrusted me with this body on earth and I need to look after it for him. And he did something very special for me as well – he sent his Son, Jesus, to die for me in pain on the cross. That to me says that God loves me lots and so, I should also learn to love myself in the same way.

In Jeremiah 1, God tells him: "Before I made you in your mother's womb, I chose you. Before you were born, I set you apart. I will be within you, speaking through you!" Jeremiah, like Moses before him, did not like the call that God had given to him. However, God wanted to be with him and so he filled him with His spirit. As Christians, if we have accepted the gift of the Holy Spirit and have Him inside us, then how can we fail to love ourselves? We have God within us.

I think the problem is that deep down inside of ourselves, we are perfectionists. If we try and do something, the phrase that comes back to haunt us is "could do better!" We always tend to think of that! We don't like to promote ourselves. We don't find it easy to congratulate each other, but we deserve it. It boosts our confidence. We ought to be satisfied with ourselves.

So, my challenge to you is to 'LOVE YOU AS YOU ARE!' After all, God made us and Jesus died for us. Surely, we are worth loving!

NIGHT VISION

We live in a crazy world where it's quite commonly believed that 'Image in Everything'! We have to have a certain image to fit in with other people otherwise we get labelled or are considered to be someone very different. Image matters in the world of pop, TV and sport. You'd be forgiven for thinking that image really did matter! But we don't always get the right view of something from the image that it portrays. A skinhead doesn't necessarily mean a thug, wearing sandals doesn't necessarily mean they're a Christian and a suit doesn't mean a professional. We stereotype – aren't we bad?

I remember my image of God was one shared with many other people. It was the long, stringy white beard and the old, fragile look of a man, who resided on this golden, shining throne on top of a wispy, yet fluffy cloud. That was the God that I grew up trying to understand and is still the view of God these days. You never know, that could be accurate, but as I grew up, I began to try to learn and understand God not for what he looked like, but for what his personality was like. How did he come across? Who was this God?

Trying to picture God is a mere impossible task – I'm not sure we can do a very good job of it, but getting to know him, in all his forms, we can. God is there for us whenever we need him. Let's get to know him as he is!

✪✪✪✪✪

NIGHT VISION

I dreamt an amazing dream once. And this is what I dreamt.

I had a visitor one night. As I lay in my bed, an angel came to me. It wasn't obvious at first that they were an angel – there were no wings, no bright T-shirt saying "I'm an angel" was being worn, but the light that shone from their face showed a heavenly glory. Plus he introduced himself as Angel Ally. I didn't know what to say. After all, he'd just entered my bedroom without opening any doors. And his first words really shocked me.

"Can you come with me? God wants to meet you."

Taken aback, I couldn't respond. Opening and closing my mouth like a fish, no words would come out. The angel just smiled.

"I know that means a Yes. Follow me."

Obediently, I followed. I didn't know what else to do. It's not every day an angel comes to you in the middle of the night.

The angel led the way down the road. I walked a few paces behind, not really sure where he was taking me. All of a sudden, he turned a corner and a bright, metallic escalator was in front of us, reaching up to the skies above. It seemed to go on forever. I stood there, gasping for air, mouth wide-open.

The angel laughed. "You haven't been able to speak yet! You may need to close your mouth soon."

I just stared upwards. The angel shook his head.

"Overawed? Dear me. Well, if you would just get on the escalator, God will meet you at the top."

And with that, the angel disappeared – right into thin air! I was transfixed now and just slowly stepped onto the first step of the everlasting escalator. It seemed to just keep on going and going. Eventually, I went through a cloud and the escalator just stopped in a round white room.

The round room was bare except for a wide-screen TV and in front of that was a large black leather armchair with a remote control just next to it. There was no other furniture or windows or in fact doors to enter. Just me, the TV, the chair and the TV controls. I decided to wait to meet God. After all, that's what the angel said.

I waited for some time, but God didn't show. Eventually, the temptation got the better of me, and I sat on the armchair and decided to see what was on Heaven's TV. I picked up the remote control which was a brilliant white colour and saw how strange it was. It had only seven buttons on it, all named with words I'd heard in church. Buttons one to six were white, but the seventh button was red and stood out. Each button had a word next to it, except for the seventh which just had a plus sign next to it. I looked around and couldn't see anyone nearby. No-one will notice, I thought. So I pressed the button for the channel marked 'Holy'.

The TV flashed into life and a picture came on to the screen. It seemed to be just a white screen, but eventually, the camera seemed to be zooming in on a distant cloud. As it got closer, I began to make out a man on a brilliant white throne with a large smile on his face. Dressed in a brilliant white suit, light just shone from him. Everything seemed to be so white. It got too bright for me.

I flicked the TV on to the second button, which said Righteous. This showed a much darker room with lots of people in it. I recognised it as a courtroom. There was a jury, and defence, and prosecution there. And right in the centre of it was the judge, who was elevated so much more than anyone else. I noticed that this judge was the same man who was on the throne before, only this time he had a white curly wig on, just like any judge, and red robes. He still had that smile on his face, despite being there with a gavel in his right hand. I watched with amazement as case after case, the defence lawyer managed to successfully stop the accused getting punished.

Eventually, I decided to switch to the next channel, which said Creator. The TV screen was full of green pictures and a stunning landscape. Beautiful trees and vibrant flowers filled the foreground, whilst in the distance were dramatic mountains and awesome horizons. There were birds singing and the sun was shining brighter than I've ever seen it before. Right at the front of this was an artist. I caught his face and it was the same man again. He was happily sitting at his easel with his palette of many colours, and painting away. The picture that he was painting mirrored exactly the landscape. Then the man began to paint a rainbow onto his canvas. As he painted it, it began to appear in the distant skyline.

Confused, I changed to the 'Lord' channel. It seemed to be like a medieval palace and there was a feast going on. Fine wines and exquisite foods filled the tables. The room was full, except for one empty chair. This chair was the largest by far and covered in velvet. The cutlery at that place was golden and it had the biggest selection of food there. Then, suddenly, the whole room stood and the face I'd begun to recognise entered the room. The artist was now dressed in majestic purple robes and had a stunning golden crown encrusted with many jewels on his head. Everyone bowed as he entered, and as he took his place, it seemed as though everyone wanted to catch his eye. They all waited for him to take his first bite. I couldn't wait as he surveyed the room regally.

I switched to 'Father' channel. There was something a bit different here. There was a small lad with a football underneath his arm. And he was shouting "Daddy, I want to play!" He looked eagerly as his dad appeared on screen. It was the regal gent, fresh faced and dressed in jeans and a sweater. The small boy looked so excited to see him, dropped his ball and ran up to hug his father tightly. His father, still smiling, picked him up and hugged him in return. The small boy asked him if he was going to play, and the father replied "Of course, son!" The boy kissed his dad's cheek and said "I love you!" The father smiled direct at the camera.

I was a bit mystified then and so changed the channel to 'Love'. A garden filled the screen, except that it was only full of roses. Nothing else, but roses. And they were so red, so bright and had flowered brilliantly. They seemed to go on forever. A gardener entered the screen and it was the same father from before. He was smiling as he knelt down to start to prune some roses. Then he picked a dozen of them and began to wrap them in some paper that he had in his pocket, so that it became a beautiful bunch. He walked down the garden and came to a door. He opened this door and standing there was a young lady. He handed them to her and she smiled. Then, behind here was a queue of thousands who all seemed to be queuing for these roses. I thought I'd change the channel.

All of a sudden, I felt a hand on my shoulder and I turned to look up. It was the man from TV – the white man, the judge, the artist, the king, the dad and the rose-gardener. He was standing next to me. He smiled at me and said "Hello friend!"

"You know me?" I replied, confused.

"Yes. Let me introduce myself. I am God."

Suddenly, it all clicked into place. I'd been watching God on TV. I'd seen him doing his roles. I looked at him.

"I think I've just been watching you on TV", I said. "Looked like a day in the life of you."

God laughed. "Yeah, something like that!"

"Seemed like loads of fun. Easy life – I'd love to be like you, to be all in white. I could be a judge."

God just looked me in the eye. I continued.

"To be an artist, to be a king, to be a loved father, to be a giver of love! You're so lucky! Must be such a fun time, being God!"

God took the remote control from my hand and turned his attention to the TV. He never said a word. He pointed the remote control at the screen and pressed the red button marked with the plus sign.

The screen was dark and it began to focus in on a man being beaten. There were soldiers all around the man using whips so hard and beating him with incredible force. Blood seemed to be everywhere. I couldn't quite see the victim's face. Then, they took the man, spat on him, ridiculed him and then marched him up a hill. At the top of the hill, they stripped him of his clothes and started to nail him to a wooden cross. As they lifted the cross, I managed to see his face. It was the face of the man in white, the judge, the artist, the king, the dad and the gardener. It was the face of the man next to me. It was the face of God and as the screen closed in, the smile had gone, there was pain, and frustration there. And it was looking straight at me.

God next to me just sighed. "I wouldn't say fun as much."

I turned to look at him and gazed straight into his eyes. The smile had returned and all I could see was love coming from his eyes. I burst into tears and fell at his feet. God put his hand on my head and I felt warmth.

"I love you!" I cried out to him. God just smiled.

"I love you too."

ROCKING AND ROLLING

I was well into my training for a preacher when I got chance to preach at a youth event. It became very exciting until I discovered the title of the evening – 'Sex, Drugs and rock'n'roll'. Isn't something nice better?

Isn't it funny that we have a problem dealing with talk about sex, drugs and alcohol? A real taboo subject! We find it's a responsibility for poor youth leaders across the country are advised to teach their young people about, but never adults. I'd love the chance to talk to a room of forty-somethings about what it says in the Bible about sex. Imagine the cringing that they'd do!

In all ages, we need to know the dangers of a 'rock and roll' lifestyle and how to guard against it. You're never too old to have an addiction problem and it's up to the church to help you deal with it whether it's taboo or not.

✪✪✪✪✪

ROCKING AND ROLLING

Sometimes, don't you just feel like an alien? You find yourself in situations that feel like you just don't fit in – you're not meant to be there. Why? Do I have a green complexion? Is my hair really that stupid? I used to be a little bit into clubbing. Saturday nights tended to be the time when you have a few drinks, go for a dance and totter back in the early hours on Sunday. However, one night at a friend's 21st birthday party, I went a bit too far in that I can't remember what happened from about 10pm until waking up the next morning. That was the final straw for me, so I decided that if I couldn't handle it, I wouldn't have any alcohol. Having a drink isn't wrong, but I thought that I should be able to control myself. Since that night, I haven't knowingly touched a drop! I'm sure someone gave me some in Greece on holiday – it didn't taste like

Orange Juice – but I haven't had any by choice. I'm aware that it makes me slightly sad – I know that it is a bit square to many a bar person who has looked strangely at my order of a pint of coke, but you know, I feel better for it!

Anyway, the history of my minor alcoholism isn't that necessary. When I gave it up, I didn't want to give up on going clubbing. So I didn't! I carried on going – but as I walked into clubs, things were different. I didn't feel like dancing because I danced like a fifties throwback! Would you know it, none of my friends could dance either. As I observed, everyone else was into dancing and really getting into the music, as well as drinking lots! And I was an alien – I just didn't fit in. I wasn't in the crowd and eventually, I didn't go as much – a choice that my bank manager rejoiced at!

Sometimes, we don't fit in and as Christians, we aren't meant to fit in. There are things that the 21st Century world has deemed good and acceptable. "Having an affair and cheating on your other half is just second nature" they say. "No sex before marriage is a thing of the past" they say. "Call yourself a virgin brings a yawn!" "Taking drugs is quite alright – make it legal" they say! "Getting paralytic is cool!" And the worrying thing is that Christians see the rest of the world doing it and get involved. Have we gone wrong?

I used to have a mate at school who was a radical Christian! He used to start religious debates and fight for the Christian corner – a good lad! Then, we'd hear him talking to the same people again, but sharing in cannabis with them – not the most positive witness ever! I've heard of Christians boasting about being 'out of it' after marathon drinking sessions! We hear of Christians again bragging of sleeping around! Who took the morals away? Seriously, I'm not actually ashamed of the fact that I waited until marriage to have sex. I know it's not cool to the world, but so what? Christians seem to be just like the rest of the world and go in for drink, drugs and sex just to be 'with it' – a real rock'n'roll lifestyle!

Why shouldn't we comply with the world and get into all this stuff? Well, of course, we are the church and we despise anything that's fun! We are real killjoys – you hear things like "look, they're laughing – that's the work of the devil!" I'm afraid that's the kind of reputation we have – so quick to say "that's wrong" or "I'm offended". Sadly, we are religious! That's not what being a Christian is all about! We don't just have to give up on something because it seems fun or exciting. But some stuff, we have to follow the guide book that advises on all sorts of things to do with sex, drugs and drink – by going against what it teaches, we are taking away a smile from the face of God who loves us – we are hurting Him. It really smarts, doesn't it, when you get hurt by someone you love and by going against the advice God has set out hurts him. It doesn't stop him from loving you, but it hurts him. So we shouldn't do it!

Sorry for spouting off about the things that you are not supposed to do and sounding a bit like a lecturer, but it's 'only cos' I want the best for you!' Yes, we are living in a world where peer pressure reigns and I'm sure many of you have been in a situation when it feels like you should be like the world, where being a Christian isn't that cool! How do we deal with peer pressure? Well, we need to stand up for what we believe in! We need to be strong in our faith and live as God wants. Easier said than done I know, but that's what being radical is all about – we need to be radical as Christians, just like Jesus!

However, we are in the world and we have to live there. But get it clear, we are in the world, but not really of the world – we've got something that makes us stand out from everyone else – we get a free gift of the Holy Spirit from God when we surrender to Him. We get that gift to help us stand up for our faith, and to live a life with God. To deal with peer pressure, we need to lean on the power of the Holy Spirit. When you are under pressure, ask what you think God wants you to do and with the Holy Spirit inside you, you can be led the right way. Even as the corny question – What would Jesus do? – and let that question be answered.

Read what it says in 1 Corinthians 6:

Do you not know that your body is a temple of the Holy Spirit, who is in you, whom you have received from God? You are not on your own – you were bought at a price. Therefore, honour God with your body!

Do it! We should honour God with our lifestyle – we should honour him with our body. Does that mean we can take drugs because friends say so? Do we drink till we are paralytic? Do we try and go out for that easy lay, just because it seems like the done thing? Is that the treatment you give to a body that's a temple of the Holy Spirit? Ask yourself that question. Live a spirit-led life!

What do we do then in the 21st century to get our kicks then? Well, I could say 'go to church', but sermons, early Sunday mornings, bible study and hymns have never sounded like the most fun thing to do. Making friends, having a laugh, and letting the Holy Spirit take you on exciting journeys is a lot more appealing. We don't have to get our kicks from other places, we don't have to get excitement from stuff that everyone else says is fun, we get our excitement from the fact that we have a Saviour who died for our sins so we can get God's riches! If you can't get your kicks from that, then you'll struggle to get a kick anywhere!

So how do we live as a 21st Century Christian? We surrender to God, build a solid relationship with Jesus, let the Holy Spirit in and have fun. Of course, we can get to live a rock and roll lifestyle, but let's make sure that it's the Holy Spirit that does the rocking and the rolling.

GO OUT
Sharing faith with people that need it

BE WISE

I don't think that there is a scarier word in the Christian sector than evangelism. I can do praying alright, I'm not afraid of preaching, even prophecy doesn't worry me. But there's something about the word 'evangelism' that brings me out in a cold sweat! Even now, writing about it is making my clothes stick and my hair get wetter. So, what is it about evangelism that gets me so scared?

It is hard, I'll accept that, to have the courage to go to someone you don't know and tell them about Jesus and your relationship with Him. Imagine someone walking up to you in the street and asking you to move to the Arctic. You'd probably laugh, unless it was your lifelong dream to be an Eskimo and live in an igloo. But that is life-changing and evangelism is doing exactly that – we want to change someone's life for the better.

It's even harder to tell someone you do know about being a Christian. They already have an opinion about you that could change within a few words. And then there is the fear, not of rejection, but of someone questioning you. How will you cope when you're put on the spot? Yep, it's a scary thing, evangelism!

But people, it's so rewarding! To see lost souls saved, to see people you love coming into a relationship with God. Is that not worth taking the plunge for? As Peter found out in Matthew 14, it's worth taking a risk, stepping out of the boat and walking. After all, God's going to help you and save you! I hope the following encourages you to be wise.

BE WISE

Sometimes in life, you learn great lessons. We learnt a great lesson about going to church once. It was a Sunday morning and as always, we were running a little late for church. We leapt into the car and drove to the place where the church met, in a school, but in fact, not that Sunday – it had been move! No-one was there, and we'd turned up at the wrong place. It had been in the notices quite a few times, but I'd never really registered it was that Sunday! Never mind – we did make it to church although really late, but if only we'd read the signs – because the real irony is that the directions issued actually directed people down the road that we live on to get to the new school!

I learnt another lesson when I did some labouring for a friend. He was so good to give me a bit of work, so I thought I'd do a good job for him. We started off on Monday morning and went to the wood yard to pick up some door frames for a barn conversion. I picked them up, loaded them in the van and then went back to the shop. As we came to leave the building, I tried to get in the van, but it was locked. He looked at me and said: "That's the wrong van!" I leapt into the front seat and it wasn't until we got on site that I realised that the door frames were in someone else's van. If only I'd read the signs on the van, I'd have realised!

If only we'd read the signs in life, we might be able to see where we are going! So many times, we get lost, we think we know best and forget to read the signs! We can walk down paths that maybe we shouldn't – all because we haven't read the signs!

If you get chance, look at some of the bright signs that churches put up to encourage people to find out more! They are on notice boards with their funny little messages that churches put out to be 'humorous!' The one that caught my eye is the one with the message:

What is missing from ch ch?
ur

I'll be the first to admit that it is very clever and there must be someone smugly reading that, gripping their lapels and nudging to their friend "I made that one!"

People will say that this is quite a radical way of advertising the church – better than nothing, and because it's a 'new' and supposedly trendy way of advertising church, it's 'cool'! I have to be honest and say that looking at the poster made me cringe! It worried me that this church's whole evangelism policy would be that sign. What are we doing to get more members? Putting up fluorescent signs, of course!

Well, we have the Bible, we have Jesus, we have the Holy Spirit within our churches, but let's be honest, we're not so great at painting all of it in glossy colours! After all, we have something exciting to share! But we've got good at hiding away! The first church, in Acts, in an upper room was hidden just like the light that Jesus talked of in Luke 8. We often take shelter under the bowl and are hiding the excitement and relevance of Jesus' death for us on the cross. We've got the truth and it's in the Bible, but we've got good at hiding it away behind our church doors.

It's a mistake that we expect people to discover the gospel and the good news from posters! Sometimes, we expect people to walk into our churches by reading a poster, by seeing the church there, or by putting our services in the paper! I think churches do that, expecting revival from it. In some ways, it might just work, but you can't beat first hand contact! We've got to be direct in sharing the gospel – we've got to go out into the world and tell people what Jesus means to us and the difference he can make to their lives!

We need a slogan for the church to follow! I've got one that could be adopted – inspired by one that filled me with horror as I sat in the Doctor's surgery waiting for my "friendly GP" to stab me in the arm so that I would be protected from the flu!

The slogan that stuck in my mind was "Be wise, Immunise." Well, let's change that slightly – the church's motto should be:

BE WISE, EVANGELISE

Our calling is to go out and spread the gospel! Let's be wise.

I think that making church look good from the outside is appealing to the eye, and a bright poster with a funny message will be good to get attention – but in so many cases, it is a false sense of advertising! You see, so many churches are full of serious faces with an unenthused worship! Are there many smiles around in your church?

I remember once having a Health and Safety inspection at work. My office was what I like to call a 'working' area because there was still work all about the place! Well, for the inspection, it was decided that my office needed a good tidy up to make a good impression! And this would me up. Not just for the fact that I had to move stuff and vacuum and get a little bit dirty. No, what wound me up about it was that my way of work was not in any way affected by what was around and about the office! I was still working the same way in a tidy office as I was in an untidy one! And all it needed tidying for was to make a decent impression on someone! Are we like that as Christians? Do we tend to put on a disguise on the way we worship? Are we seen as grey people or are we alive and burning with the Holy Spirit? And if we are, do we show it in worship? Do we portray church as a house of love where Christians can meet and feel refreshed? Or is it a place where newcomers feel uneasy, lost and unwelcome? I know which was God welcomes his people! Which way do you?

Let's be brave, let's be passionate, let's be Spirit-led – and most importantly, "Be wise, evangelise!"

ONIONS

I wish everyone was like me – the world would be a much more comfortable place. People would actually understand me, instead of frown at me or distance themselves. People would know just what it means to be excited about a non-league football team, to take playing on a tennis computer game as a be all and end all, and people would understand exactly what was in my head...

That's a worry – I wouldn't want people to know that! People would know what my opinion of them was, or that when I was talking to them, I was thinking about something completely different. People would know my cynical thoughts as well as my positive ones. I'm glad I'm different and no-one is anything like me!

We've never really grasped being united in church – we've never really understood our differences. I've been present at various ecumenical functions where it's been said that Mrs Smith hasn't come because she doesn't like the Baptists, or Mr Jones doesn't like the way the Methodists do things, so he's not here. Aren't we all following the same God? We just choose to do it differently.

Even within your own church, there can be divisions and people not getting on with each other. Squabbles, fights, petty disputes! What a glorious day when the church is working together!

Ecumenicalism – "One Body, One Lord!"

ONIONS

I am an onion! Everyone else I know is an apple! It's not fair! A lone onion in a world of apples! Actually, I'm hoping for some support here, because I'm sure that I'm not the only one. There's a saying that goes:

**'Different people have different opinions,
Some like apples and some like onions!'**

It's a terrible rhyme, but it's true.

We all have different opinions on lots of things! Look below – I wonder if you can pick one of these. You have choice to make. Here we go:

Which do you prefer (and you have to choose one – you get splinters by sitting on the fence!)

**Kylie Minogue or Britney Spears?
Brad Pitt or Fred Astaire?
Playstation or Playschool?
Balamory or Balaclava?
Mum or Dad? (Just kidding!)**

See – it's true – we are all different! Can you honestly say that someone's exactly the same as you? Excluding identical twins, of course!

We are all different – we have different ideas, different body shapes, different heights, different hair colours and different hobbies. We are definitely different! Do you know what, God thinks that's perfect! He doesn't want everyone to be the same – he likes it when we are all different. It makes it more interesting for him!

Church really only works when lots of different people come together and make it happen. If a church was just a bunch of clones, with all the same likes, styles and even the same faults, it would be an awful place! We're not like that – fortunately! We have lots of different people together and that makes church marvellous!

Paul says in 1 Corinthians 12 about having different people in church and it's from the completely unauthorised version of the Bible:

Now the body is not made up of one part, but many! The foot says: "No way! I'm not a hand! Look at that smarmy hand up there – it gets to scratch, brush, shake, point and wave, and what do I do? I just kick and walk – how boring! The hand – it's so special!" Then the hand says: "But I can't kick and walk – you're so lucky!" And the foot says: "Oh yeah! I am special!"

Then the ear says: "Look at that cheeky eye – it winks, it blinks, it can look up and down and gets to see everything! What can I do? I can just hear!" And the eye says: "But I can't hear! You're so lucky!" And the ear says: "Oh yeah! I am special!" Where would the body be if all we had was a hand, or all we had was an eye! The body needs many parts to function as a whole body, just like the church needs many people to make it great!

Sometimes, though, people think that they are not part of the church. They feel useless and because they aren't like someone else, they feel that they aren't a vital part of the church! That's very, very wrong! To really work, church needs leaders, readers, stewards, sweepers, and washer-uppers! All sorts of different folk to make the place work! Churches would be some place if it was just full of leaders and no-one able to make the tea. There'd be too many chiefs and not enough Indians saying "How?" Funny, that would be the question that we would be asking. How does a church work with so many chiefs? Simple – it doesn't! We need a small number of chiefs and lots of Indians.

I worked at an event in Manchester once and it showed just a little bit about what happens when you throw together lots of different people from all over the country – all with different accents, different backgrounds and different gifts. What happened is that they took a portion of Geordies, a sprinkling of Cockneys, a dollop of Brummies and one nut and plonked them all in the middle of Manchester with God giving them a stir! God worked through so many different people to do something that has changed parts of Manchester forever! Not with a team of mirrored people, but with a team of many parts working as one body.

The church is the same. We have different faces, different gifts, but if we can work together as a team, we can make a change through the church and make the world really see that we are a great team with Jesus at the centre! Because, by using all the different parts – us! We may be different, but we are all one body!

BLESSYA

'Now may the blessing of God the Father, the Son and the Holy Spirit, go with you every day, Amen.'

They taught me well in preacher training and that was what I learnt as the blessing. It almost feels wrong if you don't do the sign of the cross, bow on one knee and sing an elongated 'Amen' on one note. That's the blessing!

Trouble is – we need to be real when we are blessing people and doing it really well. How good would it be if people of the world were genuinely "blessed" with the presence of Christians, walking along side them and helping them on their ways? That would be exciting!

Or am I just going on again like a madman talking to himself? It's very hard to tell.

"Ah well, bless him – he tries hard!"

✪✪✪✪✪

BLESSYA

Sometimes, in life, things are just a little bit predictable and things seem to be consistent! Is that true? I find that I tend to wake up at the same time every day – don't know how that happens. I always manage to wake up at about 8.30am every morning, whether weekday or weekend. Once, at a festival, I went to bed at 3.15 in the morning, and lo and behold, I was awake again at 8.30 come the following morning – or really the same morning!

I've become predictable! On a shopping trip, it becomes obvious that we will buy various things – we decide to be new in our clothes buying and then end up buying completely the same thing! I used to treat my wife to flapjack as a food treat, but now, if I've got a treat for her, she tends to know what it is. We are so predictable! Sadly, it's the same at church! We do things the same way – we like to be consistent and do things in a regular way! If you've ever seen the film 'Groundhog Day', it feels like life has got like that!

I think that if I write something, you'll know exactly what will follow. Be honest with yourself. I'll write the word and you think what you'd say next. The phrase goes:

'Atchoo!'

And everyone replies:

'Bless You!'

Correct. Did you guess it?

That's what I want to concentrate on! Every time you sneeze, someone is bound to say the words "Bless You!" which is very polite. However, it slightly irks me when people say that! I believe that it stems from an 'old wives tale' when they used to believe that by sneezing, a person was evicting demons and evil spirits! I don't think that's true otherwise the police would be going round jails stuffing powdered pepper up every criminal's nose! It's an interesting phrase, though, and you hear it a lot!

You also hear it when people greet a brand new baby or a small child. People will peer into a pram and look at the baby by going "Aah – Bless him" or "Bless her"! And that's a bit better – we should bless little ones! Also, you tend to hear 'Bless you' when you are referring to some sort of idiotic behaviour – I've been around at a lot of places and heard the phrase "He's as thick as two short planks, bless him!" What exactly does that mean?

That is the question – what exactly does it mean? We have these phrases in the world – both 'Bless You' and a common one – 'God Bless'? They are used so often! Why do we use such terminology? I very often sign off messages – emails and text messages – with the phrase 'God Bless'. I only started using that recently and I do mean that when I do that, I'm actually asking God to bless the lives of those that I'm sending a message to. I want God to be part of their life and I think that when we say 'God Bless', we do mean that! We do want God to be in our lives and to be in the lives of those that we send those regards to. At least, I think that's what it's supposed to mean. When we say 'Bless You', we are asking the same. We want their life to be blessed - we are saying that we want God to touch their lives in only the ways that he knows how! So to you, dear reader, I say "God Bless!"

So often, I think that we tend to overlook that fact – we are very quick to say 'bless you' without think about what we are saying! We are asking that God's Spirit rests upon them and becomes part of someone. It's such a casual two words that has become misused. I think that's why saying 'Bless you' frustrates me! When someone sneezes, I believe that we tend to, out of habit, automatically say 'Bless you'! It has been something passed down from generation to generation without making a thought for what we are actually doing – what we actually mean! It has become predictable, consistent and a tradition!

Perhaps that's what certain elements of church are – things that have become passed down from generation to generation and picked up as habit, as tradition! We can do things without actually thinking about them, second nature, without actually taking stock and remembering that we are actually a house of worship, a body of worship for the one true living God who reigns over all the earth. Too often, I look back and believe that we have become a church that is governed by its rules, its predictability, its habits and traditions. God's not obsessed by habits, Jesus was so radical that he went against many traditions of the day and the Holy Spirit takes on so many forms that he could never be described as being predictable. How did we get to that stage? How did a Spirit-reliant church that began with an outbreak of inter-continental conversation become a place where boundaries reign, where the vibrant colourful Gospel is hidden away and where someone who escaped from a water-tight tomb is now restricted to a box?

I think it stems partly back to those two words – 'Bless you!" The church has been full of people and it's still true today, who are only interested in what they get – if they don't like something that goes on, then it's terrible! I think that's mainly where denominations came from – people not being satisfied of what goes on in a church, whether they get chucked out of do the chucking themselves. The church is crying out for people who will be able to say 'Bless you' to each other! Not when you sneeze, not when you're an idiot of when you're a cutie, but bless someone when they need blessing. Then, to make it complete, bless that person when they don't need blessing. What I mean by that is not by saying 'Bless you, brother' but bless someone by your deeds, by taking time out to be interested – to go the extra mile! One thing I imagine, and let me make it clear that it is me, is that we can pray for comfort in someone's life, and God turns round and says "well, I've given you the tools – go comfort them!" It may be difficult, but we, as a church, are called to bless people and we can do that by serving them aiding in their needs.

In John 13, Jesus got down on his knees and washed the feet of his disciples. As a master, he served them. Even in the muck of several days travel, when feet would absolutely stink and would look terrible – no matter how icky or disgusting, Jesus got down and served his disciples. He never whinged or shook his head, but obediently, got down to serve. Then, on Good Friday, he went even further and died on a cross for us. He was willing to go the extra mile to bless his people – he was willing to do what it takes to serve us and to bless us! If that's what the man who we, as Christians, follow was prepared to do for each of us, surely we can do that for our fellow church members. He set an incredible example – we need to do the same.

Can we honestly say that today's church is a place where people serve each other? Is it a place where harmony is in charge, where you can truly say that people bless each other?

You could say "yes", but it wouldn't be true. You may think of your close friends in church, the cliques, your social friends and say "Yes, we serve each other" but, on the whole, the 21st Century church always has niggles between people. There must be people in church that you don't get on with, that 'do your head in' so to speak, and whatever ideas they have, you dislike them and there is confrontation. Is that the kind of church we want? Do we want a church full of people that are only interested in what affects them?

We can't be blamed – we live in a society that is selfish and always focused on the individual. We need to know what we can get out of things. People always want more money, possessions or comforts to try and fill up unsatisfied hearts and souls. One of the things that annoys me is the debate for using fairly-traded coffee. I know it's my own view, but I was at a meeting where people couldn't understand the benefits of paying a bit more for their coffee to guarantee those in the third world getting a fair wage. The argument against that was that they wouldn't make as much profit from their coffee mornings! I don't think that needs any further comments except that I think that is evidence that we live in a selfish world!

Paul, in Ephesians 4, is pretty clear. He wanted the church to be a place where people can be built up. A place where there was no bitterness, no rage or anger, no slander or brawling. He wanted a place where people were kind and compassionate to each other and a place where people forgave each other. That was a message that the church in Ephesus needed to hear, but is still relevant today – we need to be a place that isn't full of malice, that doesn't put people down, that is warm, understanding and a place where people can feel blessed to be in it.

The world is a place where people get knocked down, but church is a place that can set an example for mankind! How excited would people be if they came to a church full of Christians who, by their deeds, stand up to forgive those that need forgiveness, are kind to those in need of kindness, are compassionate to those that need compassion and make church the place that truly says to the world 'Bless you!'

To do this, I thought I'd write an acronym that I think 'Bless' means:

Bring
Love and
Encouragement from
Sunday to
Sunday

That's what we need to do to really bless each other, to be the ones kneeling at other people's feet ready to serve no matter how dirty the job and do it every day. I can't say it any better that that! That is our mission – to bring love and encouragement from Sunday to Sunday!

Let's make this place one where people can be encouraged – let the Holy Spirit lead us to fill someone with words of love, kindness and compassion. Words that will be a blessing! That's what a place that Jesus reigns in should be like.

Let's say to the world 'Bless you' and mean it! Let's make sure that the world can feel warmth from the things that we do, feel strength from the encouragement we give. Then maybe, just maybe, they can feel excitement from the Gospel that we've got – one that's just not so predictable! And let's be a church that lifts Jesus high through the way that we bring love and encouragement from Sunday to Sunday!

HEAVEN SENT
What did Jesus say?

RIDING THE WAVES

I remember on my honeymoon of sitting on the side of the boat, legs dangled over, and enjoying feeling the sea coming up onto my legs. Everything was so calm, so peaceful and so beautiful that I couldn't possible think about feeling at risk.

I suppose I was though. The boat could have toppled and I could have been struggling in the sea. We never know what we're going to hit the storms.

The good thing to know is that we are never alone! We have a great deal of help with us and that keeps us going. Jesus never leaves us and is riding the waves with us when we fall in.

Let's go surfing, then!

✪✪✪✪✪

RIDING THE WAVES

Denmark! It's famous for lots of things. Like Wonderful, wonderful Copenhagen. And Hans Christian Andersen. Great Danes. Pastries. Bacon! Makes me hungry!

The reason that I wanted to look at some of the great things about Denmark is because I want to tell you of something from the other end of the Danish scale. I don't want you thinking that I'm anti-Dane because I'm not, but I want to remind you of a Danish export to England. Now, back in the year 1017 (not that I'm expecting anyone to remember it!), Denmark started to rule Britain. The very first ruler from Denmark was a man called King Canute. I'm sure you remember why Canute is a famous name from history – probably because he's more infamous and well-known as a tragic ruler. Well, Canute let power go to his head and decided that he was the most powerful man in the world. One day, he got his loyal, but probably mystified, henchmen to carry him in a daft chair down to the beach and let him sit there so that he could tell the waves to stop – at his command! As if! The waves lapped at his feet, engulfed his chair and left him with egg on his face, giving his henchmen much hilarity I'd imagine!

Anyway, you don't hear much else from King Canute apart from that, unsurprisingly. That was his moment. But he isn't so much of an idiot. I used to run a football team and when it got to a Friday night, I'd be looking at the weather thinking "Now, don't even think about raining tonight, I don't want to call off the match tomorrow." Have you ever been doing something important, like the garden or going for a walk, and you've told the weather to hold off? I'm sure you have! But think, do you reckon that because every time it was grey, and I told it not to rain, the sun came out? Never – and I had to call off numerous matches, because, frankly, the weather never listened! Or was it more likely that I don't have the power to tell the weather to stop? I think that is altogether a more likely scenario!

When we look at the story of Jesus calming the storm in Matthew 8, the thing is Jesus does exactly that. He rebuked the wind and the rain of the storm and immediately, everything was still. No Canute-style embarrassment but a furious storm completely stilled by the word of Jesus. It shows that Jesus is incredibly powerful man! As the disciples exclaimed, "even the wind and the waves obey him!"

I know it's the kind of story that we have probably grown up with, but let's take stock a moment. Now, what the bible doesn't say is that whilst the disciples were in the boat, it started to drizzle and a bit of a breeze started. It says that a furious storm blew up. You may get some idea from all the hurricanes in the USA. I don't think it would be as powerful as those, but certainly not like anything we experience in the UK. Lake Galilee was very particular to sudden violent storms being in a basin surrounded by mountains. Now, imagine this storm – it would certainly be frightening for the disciples and to top it off, throughout this storm, the man they followed, the man they called teacher was napping!

I'd be petrified and I completely holy sympathy with the disciples. They panicked, they shouted and eventually, they woke Jesus up! "We're going to drown!" Then Jesus replied, "Oh ye of little faith" and calmed the storm completely. With his word, the storm just went from being full of violent, crashing waves, pouring rain and furious winds, to being calm, relaxed and I can imagine that a rainbow would appear. An amazing experience, but I think suddenly, they'd be shocked as to how powerful Jesus actually was and also, questioning who he was.

Jesus had done miracles and healings before, but now he was dealing with the weather, something that mankind had no control over. I think that the disciples would be totally overawed by what he had just done. Even more so by the fact that he had just said "Stop"! From their history, they would know that Moses has stopped water with a rod, Joshua with the Ark of the Covenant, and even Elisha with a cloak, but Jesus just said a word and it all became calm. They would know, from reading the Psalms, that only God had power over the wind and the waves. The disciples, realising this, said "What kind of man is this?" not wanting to accept that this man with them was God. After all, he was so human! Apart from being a teacher, he did things as humans did, just like them. To them, he seemed too human to be able to do God things. He would be with them, washing like they did, getting thirsty, even needing to rest sometimes. Just so human! In fact, seconds before calming this storm, he'd been asleep, just like you and I would have been hours ago.

Sometimes, we forget things like the fact that Jesus was human, because he was so powerful. I have an issue with the song "Away in a Manger", and in particular, the line "But Little Lord Jesus, no crying he makes!" How daft! Jesus was a baby – of course, he cried, he needed burping, he'd be hungry, he needed to sleep and he needed a nappy. He'd probably scream the stable down! But even with those human characteristics, he was God and did have power including over the elements. In a way, it's almost like having your hero sitting on the subs bench at your favourite football team. It just doesn't seem right and so unnatural! Jesus was God and human.

He went through life and demonstrated his God-given power across the land performing miracles, healing and teaching, until what happened in Jerusalem!

What Jesus did on the cross was the ultimate sacrifice for us. The same man who could stop the wind and the waves couldn't save himself from death on a cross. He died, but he died importantly for each one of us. He went through a painful human crucifixion, and suffered great agony. As the Kendrick song The Servant King, says: "Hands that flung stars into space to cruel nails surrendered!" Yet, despite apparently surrendering on the cross, he proved his almighty power just three days later by defeating something else that was only controlled by God – death! The cross was the ultimate showing of God's power and also, his great love for each one of us.

Jesus did die on the cross for us. In Colossians 2, we read that 'God has reconciled us by Christ's physical body through death to present us holy in his sight, without blemish and free from accusation.' Basically, for the cross, we are forgiven and right with God. That is the wonder of getting to know Jesus – if we accept him for who he is, our Lord, our Saviour, our sacrifice to God, we are made right in God's eyes. Jesus says: "I know him" or "I know here, I died for them!" So human, yet so godly – and so powerful. We really need to thank him for the cross and hear the gospel and tell the world about him.

Knowing Jesus is so vital in the storm. Sometimes in our lives, we can feel the effects of a storm and Jesus is there for us. Not just our saviour, but our friend. I don't know what the storms are in your life, but let me share with you one thing from my life.

When I was 15, my dad became ill for the second time with cancer. The first time it had been OK – he had treatment and got better. This time, doctors were more pessimistic, they weren't hopeful and a few months later, it was to be the last few days before my dad died. I was a bit lost, confused, didn't know where to turn. I wanted to scream, to declare that life is unfair, to take it out on whoever I could and generally blame life for the bad times. I won't be the first person who feels like that and I certainly won't be the last. How could it be fair that a youngish man, my dad, could be taken away? What was God playing at? To be fair, a furious storm was brewing and ready to rain on down.

My dad did die, but it never ever rained down enough though, and I never did scream, shout and make a fuss on how life had treated me unfairly. I just calmed down and, not meaning to sound arrogant, took it in my stride. A storm had raged down and on reflection, a pretty furious one, but it had been calmed and now I realised the reason why. I had a Saviour who loved me, and had blessed me enough to calm the storm. I've seen many people in a similar situation to mine, and who have not had the storm calmed, maybe because they didn't turn to Jesus in the tough times. I have a friend who can help me through the storm though – Jesus!

When you become a Christian, tough times aren't meant to disappear and life just doesn't get easy because you follow Jesus. He will be able to be the power in your life and be able to share the peace in and after the storm.

Think in your life, when things have been tough for you and believe me, they are allowed to be. Sometimes, we believe that everything has to be happy, smiley and nothing ever goes wrong. We pretend to be perfect people, but that is purely a fantasy. Someone who seems forever happy is still every now and then dealt a rough blow which leaves them bubbling away inside at times with sadness, with trials to get through. You do have to have the rough to really appreciate the smooth. Church should help. If life was a race, the church shouldn't be the one that runs out in front of the pack shouting out "Look at me, I'm a shining example!" I pray that the church should be the ones right at the back offering a shoulder to those that need it and maybe, even piggy backs to the stragglers in the race of life.

So, I'm sure that your life at some point has had low times. Think of that time – maybe you have had physical problems, illnesses or accidents, depression, relationships gone wrong, maybe doubt, a time when you didn't want to carry on, a time when you were reduced to tears because it's certainly a crime not to cry – emotions can be shown. Are you at that place now? I want you to use your imagination now.

You are in a boat in the middle of a lake all alone, in darkness, and the storm is coming down – torrents and torrents of rain pouring down all over you and all your clothes are drenched. You can barely move. There is an icy wind blowing right into your face, it's making your eyes water, it is cutting into your face and it stings. Crashing waves seem to be coming over the side of the boat from every direction and filling the floor below – you fear you are going to drown – salty water is all you can taste on your lips. There is no hope – the storm is getting too much – you decide that you can't cope and you kneel in the middle of the boat, head bowed, eyes closed. It's time to give up! And then, all of a sudden, there is nothing. Rain has been replaced by a sun beating down on the back of your neck. The wind is no more and the sea is calm. As you stand, a hand touches your shoulder. It's Jesus. You look at him. He smiles and exclaims "It's all over!" "I could have drowned" you scream. "Correction – we could have drowned, but we didn't!" I was there all the way through to make sure we got through it! I always will help you through every storm – just turn to me and we will see it through!" As I turned, I saw a rainbow across the sky with the words 'we made it' written across. Jesus is powerful enough to see through any trouble. No matter what storms life can throw at you, having Jesus as part of your life will see you through them. He won't always calm them immediately, or in the way that you want, but he will be with you in every storm making sure that together you see it through.

In a similar way, we as a church are in a boat riding on a sea that throws up storms. Every now and then, we have to deal with trials. We, like the disciples, have Jesus at the centre ready to help us, but most importantly, going through it all with us. He is the most powerful.

So, I have a simple challenge for you. If life does get on top, if you feel like it's too tough, if you need help, turn to Jesus. He is powerful enough to weather the storm. Always turn to him. He is also ready to help you through the storm and be with you in the aftermath – right the way through until you can see the rainbow on the other side because there is always one on the other side. After the storm comes the calm, with Jesus exclaiming: "With me, every little thing's gonna be alright!"

BARKING UP THE RIGHT TREE

Where would the world be without controversy? You wouldn't get the press gangs salivating at the chance to print something out of the ordinary, you wouldn't get TV stations broadcasting stories over and over again and you wouldn't get people having fans following them waiting for the next defining moment.

The more famous you are, the easier it is to be controversial. Some people in the public eye only need to change their washing powder or say they like a certain brand of chocolate to make the media take it out of context. They want to make it more and more controversial.

I love controversy! I like debates and I like to hear points of genuine different opinions to be argued without resolve. I think controversy starts that! And I'm glad that the one I follow was often controversial, speaking against the ways of the leaders of the day. He stood up for what he believed in and not for controversy's sake either!

Controversy and Christianity – I'm glad they go together!

✪✪✪✪✪

BARKING UP THE RIGHT TREE

You can't beat a bit of controversy. It would be a bit daring to go with something a bit controversial. Ah well, here goes.

If I was to give a word to you, what would your reaction be? Racist. It's a taboo word, isn't it?

Some people have made a career by being racist – telling jokes against all sorts of minorities and in fact, anyone who is not a true Brit! It's something that is very evident in the world today and something that is rife!

So my question to you is how does that link with Jesus? Is he a racist? I'm afraid that at times, if he lived in the Politically-correct world that we live in today, the answer would probably be 'Yes!' Before you shoot me down, it's not the kind of racism we see today. However, in Mark 7, we read of the Gentile woman coming to Jesus that initially, he appeared not to want to heal her. She had a sick daughter and Jesus basically said that he was here to save the Jews – he didn't have powers to help anyone else. She was clearly different and Jesus wanted to have nothing to do with helping her. Racist? It's a bit harsh, eh?

Imagine would you, for example, planning a summer holiday to Paris and getting to the airport in Paris. Mmmm! It's hot, you go to your hotel – and relax. The next day you get to go to the Eiffel Tower, the Arc D'Triomphe and the Notre Dame. However, as you get your taxi, the driver says "Where to?" You say all of the places and he says "I'm sorry, they are for Parisians only. Please stay in your hotel – it's not for you!" You'd be quite annoyed – being denied the chance to see some of the world's greatest sights just so the people of Paris can keep them to themselves. Of course, they wouldn't have become so famous and spectacular if they hadn't been seen by people all over the world and talked about and shared by the people of Paris.

Jesus was quite clear to the Gentile woman. "My power is for Jews only! You don't buy bread for your children and give it to the dogs." Fortunately for all of us, the Gentile woman was clever and said: "But surely Jesus, even a small amount of your power can be for us – even the dogs can lap up the crumbs from under the table." She was clever, but I can imagine her saying that quite desperately. After all, she had a daughter possessed by a demon and Jesus as her last hope. Topped off with a straight refusal and being referred to as a dog, she'd be quite annoyed! But Jesus recognised her wisdom and heard her plea, and in turn, healed her daughter.

The story really doesn't put Jesus is such a good way, but he was right to say what he did and right to refuse to help her.

Why should he use God's power to heal someone who doesn't follow God? But the Gentile woman believed in God's power and believed that Jesus was God's son and that he had healing powers, so Jesus healed her daughter.

So where does that leave us? Well, it just goes to show that Jesus was for God's people, leaving non-believers out in the cold. The Gentile woman had to acknowledge that Jesus was the Son of God to experience his power. There is little change for us in today's world. We can't expect to receive the power of God's Holy Spirit if we aren't willing to open ourselves to him. Do you accept Jesus as your Saviour and the true Son of God? If you do, then he will pour out his blessing on you.

Jesus was a great healer and used God's power for many healings, but he didn't restrict himself to the temples of the day. He wasn't always welcome at the temples after all, but he did his miracles on the streets and in the towns. His power and his miracles were welcome anywhere. Jesus ignored the traditions – he mixed with the beggars, the sinners and the social outcasts of the day. He mixed with and even helped people of other religions – like the Gentile woman. He clearly carried out God's work in the full light of everyone around – they could all see him doing miracles! He was radical, dealt with realistic situations, and was relevant to the way things were. Today, Jesus Christ is still radical, realistic and relevant which means we have to be the same. We have looked at our ways of communicating with God and the world and we have to be relevant. Jesus was realistic in the way he dealt with the Gentile woman and we too have to be realistic with the way we treat people. But radical?

Radical is the kind of word that makes some traditional Christians cringe! What has the church got to do with being radical? Why not keep it as it's always been?

Being radical is about dealing with the fundamentals,
Making reforms,
Changing,
Breaking away from the norm,

It's about wearing a nose ring,
Dying your hair,
Shaving your head,
It's about preaching in the streets,
Fasting for a month,
Helping the poor,
Standing up for God
It's about healing the sick,
Befriending the sinners,
Raising the dead,
DYING ON A CROSS!
Then coming back to life!

Was Jesus not the greatest radical of all time? It needs no question, he was. We, as followers of Christ have to be just as radical. We have to do things to change the world, we have to stand up for morals and make Jesus' name so high! We have to want to change history. We don't want to keep ourselves hidden behind our church doors. "But the real world is so tough – things outside are so difficult. Society frowns upon Christians!" Well, let me take you on a journey. Here we go – from Birmingham to Land's End. Past Birmingham – brrrrm – near to Bristol – screech – oops, traffic jam – we're off again – and through Devon, and into Cornwall – and here we are at Land's End – stop! Imagine your cosy car – it's windy and raining outside. So you switch on the radio, shut the windows and turn up the air con to very hot! Nice and comfortable – good. And then, after an hour in the car park, you drive all the way back to Birmingham. The next day, you tell all your friends about how you've been to Land's End. Have you really been?

After all, you sat comfortably and looked out upon it from your car. You need to go that extra yard – yeah, it's raining and windy – the cliffs could be dangerous and slippery, but only after you have walked the cliffs, felt that rain and wind beating on your face and left the car in the car park can you truly say that you have been there and fully experienced it. You have actually been to the limit.

Our Christian path is exactly the same – we need to leave our comfort zones and then we can genuinely share our stories. God calls us to difficult situations – that seem horrid, that are scary and that are definitely not something we've got planned. But if God calls us, we go! We push the barriers and endless possibilities occur. We once had evening events on in Manchester at a site where two rival areas would meet – there was a Christian concert with a gospel message incorporated. Thousands came and yet there were armed police, fights breaking out, bricks thrown at people, drugs and alcohol, but you know what had more presence that any of them – God's Spirit. Hundreds became Christians for the first time – God breaks down any barriers that he wants to!

He's calling you to do the same – push out the boundaries that restrict your faith. Share your testimony with a friend at work, spend an hour helping those that are needy, be radical, be different and be filled with God's love and Spirit. If you think it's too tough, persist and keep going – it was tough to die on a cross.

Here's a possible extract from the diary of John Wesley, the founder of Methodism, as he travelled around.

Monday	Preached in the town square - ran out of town.
Tuesday	Preached in village market – pelted with rotten fruit.
Wednesday	Preached in a field – farmer turned his bull on me.
Thursday	Preached on a village green – threatened with jail.
Friday	Preached in a field – 10,000 people turned up to hear me.

The rewards will come for those who push out their barriers.

To end, we go back to Cornwall. As you enter the car park, you see Jesus saying welcome. As you get to the water's edge, you feel a tap on your shoulder and it's Jesus. You turn and he says "Well done! You were brilliant. You've worked so hard to get down to the water's edge!"

"How did you get down here?" You ask Jesus.

"Well I was behind you all the way!"

And he always will be.

ACCEPTING GRACE

It is tough for us to understand sometimes how much it took for Jesus to face the cross and really give himself for us. We can often just accept that it happened and celebrate its greatness. For some reason, a lot of controversy surrounds graphic depictions of the crucifixion, but they tend to be the most accurate.

Jesus knew what his role on earth was and what he was meant to do for us. I would think that he wrestled with the idea of dying for mankind and found it difficult. He pleaded with God for another way in the Garden of Gethsemane in Matthew 26 before he was captured.

However, because he was actually crucified, Jesus enabled us to get Grace. What is grace though? Well, I've always loved the acronym based on Ephesians 2:1-9. Grace is summed up perfectly. It says:

God's **R**iches **A**t **C**hrist's **E**xpense

How could we sum it up any better? Through Jesus and what he did on the cross, we can get the riches that God provides. It's an exciting life for Christians!

It's key to reflect on this excitement in terms of Jesus' actual sacrifice. This poem, based on Jesus' realisation of Grace, helped to sum up this sacrifice for me.

ACCEPTING GRACE

Hey there Dad, it's me, your Son
I'm here, I'm down on earth
I've got a question, a puzzling one
That's been niggling me since birth

It's about a gift that humans get
It's talked about in every race
And everyone that I've ever met
Is craving some of your grace

Hey God, Hey Dad, your head's gone down
Please look me eye to eye
Why does your forehead bear a frown?
Why do your tear ducts cry?

What is this grace that they all crave?
What does it mean for them?
They talk of someone that has to save
How do they get it then?

You'll send forgiveness, hey, that's great
A super plan to hatch
Hey Dad, your shoulders did deflate
Go on – tell me, what's the catch?

To get your grace – a cost incurred
Death for God's son, I see
Well that's not bad, it's just... my word
Your son, Hey God, that's me!

I'm gonna die for all these folk
Be nailed to a tree
Come on Dad, is this some joke?
No, you're staring seriously.

So grace for them means death for me
I hardly think that's fair!
But Dad, that's an almighty fee
Will these humans really care?

Will they see the cost when they get grace?
Of what I had to do
Or will they forget to always embrace
Or will they have a clue?

It's your riches at my expense
I'll love them enough to die
I hope this grace makes real sense
And answers the question why?

EASTER PROMISE
Good Friday to Great Sunday!

TAKING IT TOO FAR

I never really got Palm Sunday when I was a kid. It seemed to be a day where people were given these rubber-feeling crosses to hold. I suppose that I didn't really know what a palm tree was and was quite afraid of donkeys after an unfortunate slip off a saddle on holiday (I rode a donkey upside down – a clever trick, I assure you!) I didn't really know much about Jerusalem either!

But, as I've grown older, I've begun to realise the significance and just what it meant to be Jesus receiving a hero's welcome. It would have been a great day if we didn't know what happened the following week. Imagine the thousands of people surrounding Jesus, shouting lots of great things – it would have been 'Incroyable' as the French would say.

If you wanted to be truly Christ-like, Palm Sunday is the day you would want to emulate. It's not likely to happen for us, but you never know. See below for the story of one man who took it all a bit literally and I'm afraid, got it a little bit wrong!

✪✪✪✪✪

TAKING IT TOO FAR

All right folks! My name is Jessie Christophe and let me tell you, I'm a very religious and holy bloke. In the past, I've been bullied for being religious. People look at me in the street, and call me "nutcase", "fruitcake", and other food-related names, but I really feel that I'm living my life just like Jesus. I try to be just the same as him and even have a wonderful collection of robes that I wear every now and then. I've had one or two problems growing a beard – but I'm sure it'll come. Don't get the stigmata, marks of the cross, for some reason, so I take to putting them on me hands and feet in biro. Just like Jesus, you see. It all makes it possible to feel closer to God. It's not happened yet, but one day, I'm sure I'll feel it. Now, I want to tell you a story about my Palm Sunday way back in the year 2000 – it was quite a day that day!

You see, I want to be just like Jesus and do just as he did. Well, aren't we supposed to be just like him? Isn't that what it says in the Old Bible? Well, anyway, I thought so and funnily enough, about three days before Palm Sunday, I was reading this story of how Jesus just decided to enter Jerusalem quite triumphantly. And so, I thought again, doesn't the Bible say that we are to be just like Jesus? And so I planned it. I decided to arrange my own triumphant entry into Jerusalem. And that way, I would definitely feel close to God.

Well, there were one or two stumbling blocks on the way. You see, I find it quite hard to get a job for some reason – I went to my last interview dressed in my best robes, but they never took me on. Anyway, so I haven't got any money, so going to Jerusalem was going to be a teeny bit of a problem for me. The dole never goes that far, and plus, I'm saving up for a DVD player. So, I did my research and as if it were planned, I found a pub in Nottingham City Centre called 'Ye Old Trip to Jerusalem'. Thought that must be right, and so I decided to go to Nottingham. So, this is how the day went. I took my Bible with me, just to keep God close, you know.

Well, it got to Saturday morning and the TV papers came out. Well, would you believe that they were showing football on the Sunday afternoon? Well, I always watch sport and so I thought, I'm not doing anything today. So I made my egg sandwiches, got my flask of lemon squash, put on my favourite light blue robe, and of course, my anorak and went and caught the 9.52 bus to Nottingham. I was sure that I was going to be so close to God. I didn't feel it, but give it time. Today was the day, I was sure.

I arrived in Nottingham at 11.45. I remarked to the person next to me that I was going to make my triumphant entry to Jerusalem. He said something that sounded like "Get Lost, Weirdo!" but he was a Northern man, so I thought that was a good luck message from Yorkshire. I said "Thanks. I'll remember you in heaven", and he said something like "Forget me! Please forget me! I can't bear spending eternity anywhere near you, you batty freak!" Northern customs, eh?

Anyway, I was in Nottingham now. Unfortunately, I didn't have any disciples to send ahead of me – I would have asked my friends to come, but I didn't have friends to actually ask to come with me. So I thought, I'm going to have to do this part myself. The problem was that Nottingham was a big city and not a countryside area, so where was I going to get a donkey from? That was resolved straight away. Just outside the city centre, I noticed this large green ride-on lawnmower sitting in someone's garden that I was walking by. Talk about a clear sign, I think. Well, they both tend to eat grass don't they? So, I climbed over the fence, which proved to be difficult in my robe and went and sat on the mower. Not quite a donkey, so I didn't feel much closer to God yet.

Anyway, a man came out of the house. He was elderly and looked quite frail. He had a frown and looked angry. He shouted out to me "What do you think you're doing?" I replied, very calmly, "The Lord needs it!" I exclaimed. I could see that the devil was working against me, and so, without further hesitation, I drove away, knocking down his fence on the way. He was shouting loud expletives at me. Sounded a bit vulgar, and he mentioned the police, but he didn't chase me and so, I was on my way into the City Centre for my triumphant entry. Still felt more worried that close to God. What if he did call the police? Oh, well, I was on a mission.

As I drove my lawnmower right through the centre of Nottingham, looking for 'Ye Old Trip to Jerusalem', I really felt the part. People were certainly shouting at me, although they didn't put coats down. They were waving too. Well, shaking their fists anyway. I felt like they were praising me, in a way.

I saw the Jerusalem pub in the distance and the lawnmower was going well. However, just short of Jerusalem, a police car pulled up in front of me and I crashed right into the side of it. The lawnmower started leaking petrol. It wasn't a pretty sight.

However, the policeman grabbed me by the anorak and said "Look, what are you doing?" I replied, prophetically "I am making my triumphant entry into Jerusalem. Can't you hear the cheering?" The policeman said "Erm, no. Just some people cursing you!" I said "Well, if they were quiet, the rocks and stones would sing!"

The policeman just frowned. "Are you insane?" I looked him direct in the eye. "God will send a sign for me." I must have done enough to be closer to God then.

At that moment, a gust of wind blew and my robes were blown right into the air, revealing everything I wasn't wearing underneath – parents rushed to cover the eyes of their children, and old ladies all around looked horrified. I really should have got dressed properly in the first place.

I never made my triumphant entry into 'Ye Old Trip to Jerusalem'. Instead, I spent the next three nights in a police cell for theft of a lawnmower, criminal damage, and indecent exposure. I was charged and then released. It was altogether very humiliating.

I can't understand it. I'm sure it said in the Bible that we are called to be like Jesus. That's what I was trying to do. Why do I feel that I didn't do it quite right? And I never felt any closer to God. What exactly did I do wrong? I think it must have been the lawnmower. Maybe I'll get a donkey for next year.

NUMBER ONE

I was once on a religious TV programme for a grand total of five seconds giving my opinion on how good a particular Christian festival was. There I was, on one of the main channels, with probably nearly a million watching and I had five seconds all to myself. It was a grand day! After that, I had many comments from local Christians who'd seen it saying wise things like "Saw you on the telly" or "Liked your TV appearance". For about a day, I felt like a celebrity and almost a hero.

Pride, undoubtedly, comes before a fall and for every second you become a hero, there's another when you are the villain. I remember playing football once and hitting a crisp 15 yard drive in a match for the local church. I don't think I'd struck the ball cleaner and for a couple of seconds, I held my hands in the air as the ball flew past the keeper. It was to be my finest goal, but that pride turned to despair as the shot hit the inside of the post flashed across the goal, hit the other post and bounced away again. We lost the match 1-0 and from seemingly being a hero, I was the villain.

To the Jews, thousands were singing Jesus' praise on Palm Sunday and then less than a week later, he'd become a villain. They wanted him dead. An amazing turn around! Holy week had completely gone from the highs of Palm Sunday to the lows of Good Friday. What are we to make of such a turnaround?

✪✪✪✪✪

NUMBER ONE

I was very young once, aged about seven years. And, like every other kid of my age, I had dreams. My dream was that I would play for England at football. I would be the star centre-forward and would score the winning goal to complete a hat-trick in the last minutes of the World Cup Final as England beat Brazil 3-2. I would be captain, lift the World Cup and collect the trophy in front of thousands of fans shouting "Cooper". Then there would be a return to England and an open top bus tour of London, where literally millions of people would be lining the streets just to get a glimpse of me. Swarms of them would be wearing their replica shirts with "Cooper – Number 9" on the back. And again, they would be shouting my name – "Cooper, Cooper!"

However, I am older now. For some obscure, I wasn't picked to play in the last World Cup for England and I'm not holding my breath for the next World Cup either. So, I'm going to miss out on my dream of hearing people cheering my name, seeing thousands line the street in a victory parade of have people wanting to just see me. I think I'm back in touch with reality now and take to living life as it is.

It is interesting though, because my dream was indeed a reality for Jesus on Palm Sunday. OK, so he didn't have an open-top bus, but people filled the streets all waving and cheering him as he went on his triumphant entry into Jerusalem. They didn't have replica shirts saying "Jesus – Number 9" on the back, but they had palm leaves from the nearby trees to wave at him and laid them out as he rode on the donkey. He had his hero's welcome. He was treated like a champion returning home, and he was celebrated like a winner. In my opinion, it was a truly deserved welcome for a worthy champion.

Do you like praise? Some people love it – they say "Praise me, come on!" But, if you are like me, you'll get praise and then you'll try and keep your head down all shy. Don't get me wrong – praise is nice, but sometimes you feel embarrassed to get it. I certainly do! It's probably that when you are praised, you are being recognised for one aspect of your personality, whereas you know exactly what you are like all the time and have a good understanding of the balance in your life of the good and the bad.

Anyway, we'll go back to Jesus. The point is that Jesus didn't sit on the donkey going "Shucks! You shouldn't have." Or hold up his and say "Stop!" He wasn't really very humble about it. He was paraded as a Champion. That got the backs of the Pharisees up. They must have been watching, going "Look at him. Who does he think he is? He thinks he's the Son of God." So they told him. "Tell your fans to shut up!"

If your image of Jesus is meek and mild, a dignified and humble man, then his response was not the most humble reply in history. He told the Pharisees that if the crown were quiet, the rocks and stones would start to sing. It's so easy to see why the Pharisees went away and plotted against him. You'd be thinking "What an ego?" But Jesus was right. He knew that he was the Son of God and worthy of all the worship. He continued into Jerusalem to have full pity for the way the city was going to fall.

Really, we are called to be as enthusiastic about Jesus as the many people in the crowd were on Palm Sunday. They were fanatical and as passionate about seeing Jesus come into Jerusalem as any pop-star mad teenager, or football-crazy lad would be seeing their favourite star. Do we get that passionate about Jesus, or do we just keep it quiet? Most of the time we keep it all to ourselves, but we shouldn't – we should be waving our own personal palm crosses and praising Jesus with a great love and passion. He is worth it!

But, what I draw your attention to is the fact that we are called to be like Jesus. You see, we are to be just like Him and to live like Him. However, we are not expected to copy him in every single way. That's not what is required.

Wouldn't it be great though to be like Jesus? To be cheered and praised and worshipped. Well, it will happen one day – one day, we will be applauded by all the believers that have gone before us. One day, we will be cheered into heaven. But on this earth, it is highly unlikely. But to be just like Jesus in that sense, it would be great – even for someone who doesn't like praise.

To be honest, if this Christian lark is about being like Jesus, just from reading the Palm Sunday story, anyone would fancy it! The whole world would be craving to be Christians. How could you resist? What do you reckon? Do you fancy living just like Jesus?

In the same week, only four days later, the Pharisees had worked really, really quickly. On Sunday, Jesus was being celebrated as the Messiah and now, in the same week, he was being arrested.

The trouble is the uncomfortable truth was that Jesus knew that this was going to happen. He knew that this was his purpose on earth. He knew that the next day, he was going to face a trial resulting in his execution on the cross.

Crucifixion is not something that we can really relate to these days, and so execution is a far more potent word. He didn't peacefully die - he was killed in a brutal, horrific, bloody, barbaric way. That was crucifixion.

In Matthew 26, in the Garden of Gethsemane, Judas had eternally decided to offer his name to backstabbers worldwide by deciding to betray Jesus. I'm sure that many of us have been betrayed in the past, whether it's in a relationship with someone, or at work, or even in our families. Wherever it is, it does hurt. We feel unable to trust anyone, you feel that the whole world's working against you and you feel used. What we mustn't forget is that Jesus was a human. The greatest example of how to live, but like you and me, he had emotions and strong ones at that. So, what Judas did really must have hurt him. He didn't like what he had to do. He pleaded with God to let him off, but God was maybe just a little bit stubborn. After all, he'd sent Jesus to the earth for a reason – to fulfil a promise.

When the soldiers came after Judas kissed him, the easiest thing for Jesus to do would have been to tell the disciples to charge and get them – fight the fight for Jesus. But, Jesus said "No!" It's not about fighting, it's not about a war, and it isn't about having an army to defend him. Jesus knew what he had to do, whether he liked it or not. His tone was subdued. "Why have you come with swords to arrest me? I'm not a thug. I will come quietly."

Jesus, in the next day or so, went through a trauma like no other ever seen. He was beaten, whipped, persecuted and the same crowd that was cheering him decided to free a robber called Barabbas, and have Jesus. I suppose that we are being introduced to the horrific and tragic world of Good Friday for Jesus. Not such a good day for him, but a great day for all mankind.

All Easter week, we hear the story of Good Friday, Jesus, dying on a cross, and the following Sunday, being raised from the dead to a new life. But what cannot be hidden is the terrific magnitude of what Jesus did. He died, not just for you and me, but for the entire human race. He took on board our sins in death, so that we can get closer to God through him.

Do we still fancy living just like Jesus? Would you fancy taking on all that happened on his amazing journey from being cheered in Jerusalem to being executed on a cross at Skull Hill? I don't expect to see anyone saying "Yes. Me please!" But Paul calls us to do that. At least, I think he does.

Paul in Philippians 2 said that we are to display the same attitude as Jesus. He made himself a servant. He humbled himself. He was obedient to death on a cross. We are to display the very same attitude as him.

Now, I don't expect anyone to go through what Jesus had to, but being a Christian is a tricky life to lead. So many people think Christians are polite people who have little fun, don't really do anything, and have issues with lots of things of society. That is inaccurate! But some Christians are like that. They sit, grim-faced, with tight lips, looking for things to complain about, trying to make innocent things to complain about, trying to make innocent things sound offensive, making people from certain social communities feel frightfully uncomfortable and, in my humble opinion, deface our image giving Christians worldwide a bad name. The people that fit into category seem to focus on being religious, but have forgotten what it means to be a Christian, because being religious and being Christian are very different.

Being a Christian is about being Christ-like, having the same attitude. I can't imagine Jesus saying "I am offended by that" for no just reason. He mixed with society's different people, not always looking to persecute them. Even in his first miracle, he never said "I will not change this water into wine. Alcohol is wrong". He was keen to be alongside people – to influence them by being with them. Christians should be helping others, be almost Christ-like, have fun, praising God, and telling the world about just how significant Good Friday is to mankind. That is the way of today's Christian – Do that and you will be able to bring a bigger smile to God's face.

We are asked to walk the path that God has set out for us, no matter how hard it gets, no matter what obstacles stand in our way. If life does get tough, remember the example of Jesus, who had a roller-coaster of a week. He is the one whose fall from grace was spectacular, but now look at him – glorified and at the right-hand side of God. Let's take time to think about the way that we are supposed to be like Jesus, and focus on him. Don't be religious; make sure that you concentrate on being a Christian – Christ-like – obedient, humble and loving.

Palm Sunday was a funny old day, but one that helped change the world – let's keep making sure that Jesus gets a hero's welcome from us!

SEEING IS BELIEVING

Doubting Thomas gets a picture taken on him that isn't always great. "The one who didn't believe enough!" That was him. Poor man who did get made an example and given a label! The doubter, eternally!

Yeah, he did need proof, but can you blame him? The following reading gives an account of his story.

✪✪✪✪✪

SEEING IS BELIEVING

One Sunday night, the disciples had a bit of a get-together in a room. They decided to lock the doors, just in case anyone of the Jews came along and tried to duff them up. Whilst they were there, Jesus came to the party, which was a bit good, really, because all the doors were locked and they weren't totally sure he was even alive. Last time, most of them had seen him, he was dead. Bizarre. Anyway, he came and said "Boys! How's it going?"

The disciples were obviously well chuffed at this and even more amazed, as well as being a tad queasy, when Jesus showed them holes in his hands and feet. Anyway, Jesus said "Boys! Listen up! Guess what? God sent me, so I'm gonna send you! Get it?" And after saying that, he put God's power in them. And he said "Here, have this! If you let someone off, then they are free! However, if you don't, they ain't free!" The disciples then had God's super power and felt pretty good. Jesus said "Ciao!"

Now, Tommy, he didn't bother to go to this get-together and so missed out on all the fun. When he saw the disciples in town, they said "Tommy! You'll never guess who we saw last night? Jesus!" Tommy said "You what? But Jesus is dead! I don't believe you!

"It's true" The disciples said. "Honest!"

"No way," Tommy said. "Unless I get to see the holes in his hands and stick my finger there and then shove my hand in the hole in his side, there's no way I'll believe you!"

"Urgh! That's a bit messy!" said the disciples. "But it's true, we swear!"

Anyway, next Sunday night, they decided to have another get-together, and this time, Tommy could make it. They locked the doors again to avoid getting kicked in, and then Jesus turned up again. Jesus said "Boys! How's it going?" And then he saw Tommy.

Jesus said "Hey up, Tommy! Look at my hands! Holes look. Here, stick your finger in there! If you do, then you'll probably know that I ain't dead! I'm real!"

Tommy looked at Jesus and said "Boss! You are the greatest! You're number one!"

Then Jesus said "It's all right for you. You've seen me, so then you know its true – I ain't dead. Those that don't see me but believe - they've got it well sorted."

Good old Tommy!

PROVE IT

Doubt – in a Church! Christians never doubt, do they? Of course, their faith is strong. They always believe and always stand firm. Doubt and Christianity don't go together.

If that's true, I must say that I've got a problem. I do doubt sometimes – is there a God that really loves me? Especially in times that are tricky, you begin to think "is it all worth it?"

Doubt means that I'm human. I've not gone to heaven and seen God face to face – I've just got a faith that keeps me going. And for the times that I doubt, I have times when I feel very close to God.

I suppose I'm riding a roller-coaster that goes up and down. When will it stop?

✪✪✪✪✪

PROVE IT!

Ever heard this statement "ELVIS IS ALIVE"?

I've heard that statement quite a bit in many different contexts – and I still find it quite strange really. You'll find that despite being a rock star and probably an educated man, he's always either working in a fast-food restaurant, or stacking the shelf at a supermarket. Forgive me if you believe that Elvis is still alive, but it always seems to be some dim-wit that has managed to sight him, and usually, in my opinion, someone who has lost touch with reality. It's the same with UFO's and aliens. You may have been a witness to a UFO, but it seems aliens always seem to 'abduct' those that are really two sandwiches short of a picnic. Or could it be possibly that those that have been abducted are living in their fantasy world rather than in reality with the rest of the world?

We, as the human race, do like to have proof. We like to have evidence – even in court cases. If someone says that they did it, there still has to be adequate proof for them to be sentenced. Think of some of the phrases that fill our society – 'Prove it!' 'Show me!' 'It had to be seen to be believed!' or the very famous one 'I don't believe it!' I remember once playing in a football match. One of our defenders had the ball hit him in the face which meant he had to go and be treated in casualty. By the time that he got hit, we were losing 3-0 with about half an hour to go. Anyway, we fluked a goal with about fifteen minutes to go and the opposition crumbled. We won the game 4-3. However, when it came to telling the injured player, he refused to believe it from us. It took a neutral to convince him that it actually was true.

I'm sure, like me, you love having proof. I like to see things to accept that they actually happen. When someone talks of a holiday, it's always good to see photos to see what people are talking about. We've heard hype about movies. People talk of how gory, or fantastic they are but I have to see it to make my own mind up. Do you love proof like me? I bet you do.

It's fair to say that we understand Thomas, in John 20, as 'Doubting Thomas'. He was the disciple who didn't have quite enough faith. It's a bit unfair on Thomas. He was still there at that time – he was loyal to Jesus, even after he'd died and he was a brave man. We go back earlier in John's gospel, Chapter 11, and read that Thomas encouraged the disciples to go with Jesus to raise Lazarus from the dead. He spoke of how that they should accompany Jesus and was willing to die with him. That doesn't sound like a very doubtful attitude if he was willing to die. He must have been fairly sure that he was going the right way. Thomas knew that the right road, the road to Jerusalem, would be quite dangerous. However, he went. He was honest too. He told Jesus that he didn't really understand what he was saying. It was Thomas, in John 14, who prompted Jesus into saying that "I am the way, the truth and the life." I think it's fair to say that, although Thomas was a doubter, he was very much a realist in the way he thought. He needed to have proof of things, he needed things to be spelt out and he was aware of what dangers laid ahead in following Jesus. Realist Thomas – sounds a bit better than Doubting Thomas.

Thomas didn't believe that Jesus had risen. He said, "Unless I've see the nail holes, put my finger where the nails were and put my hand into his side, I will not believe!" To be honest, I know it's not very nice of me, but that does sound like a challenge. Thomas is challenging the disciples, who he's spent the last three years with, saying that he'll only believe them if something very unlikely can happen. In a word, he said "I don't believe you!" He set down a task that even they hadn't done. They'd only seen Jesus, not touched him. Can you honestly imagine sticking your hands into another man's wounds, unless you are a doctor? Sorry. If you've ever been ten-pin bowling, sometimes you can leave two pins standing up, at opposite ends of the triangle. The chances of hitting both the pins and knocking them down are zero, but you can guarantee that some wise man says "I'll give you a tenner if you can get them both down!" It's a very cocky statement and one that will not happen. That's the sort of impression I get from Thomas. In his mind, unless he could do the very unlikely act of reaching inside a live human being, then he will not believe. He nonchalantly left it at that. He was right in his eyes, and he needed the proof. He needed to be an eyewitness.

However, Thomas, with his big statement, was sure he was right. But Jesus had other ideas, and to be honest, it would be a real sight to see Thomas' face on the night that Jesus came. Jesus knew what Thomas had said, what challenge he had laid down to the disciples and offered to let him stick his hands in the holes on his hands and his side. You can tell Thomas wasn't entirely serious about his request to do that. He just saw Jesus and called him "My Lord and My God!" That's a pretty high statement and a real compliment to call Jesus something like that. Thomas is recognising Jesus as God.

Really, you can't blame Thomas for doubting. He was being asked to believe in a man who he'd been with for three years, who he knew had died in agony, was now alive and risen from the dead. We've already ridiculed the folks that claim to have seen Elvis and that he's alive and working in a fast-food restaurant. Yet, we celebrate Easter as the day that Jesus defeated death and came back from the dead. Isn't that purely the same thing?

I like to think of myself as a realist – I deal with life in a realistic way, rather than in a fantasy world. And I believe that Elvis died and has been dead ever since. Yet, I believe in my heart that Jesus Christ on Easter Day, got up from the grave, folded his grave clothes and went out again into the world again for the second time to empower the disciples and ascend into heaven. I haven't seen Jesus in the flesh, but I know that Jesus Christ is alive today. After all, if Thomas, not at all optimistic, a realist and an initial doubter of the resurrection believes in it, and can accept that Jesus is God, then it makes it very believable.

Paul says in 1 Corinthians that if Jesus' resurrection isn't true, then surely today's preaching is totally useless. And in fact, so is your faith. The question that always gets asked is how? In a proof-craving society, we need solid proof. How do we get solid proof of the fact that Jesus Christ was raised from the dead and is living today? Do we say "Trust me!"? How do we prove it?

We have the Bible, which is a transcript of what happened at the time of Jesus. There's some proof for you! What folks today want is an eyewitness account of what is going on. They want to see, to experience for themselves and have it in right in front of their eyes. So, where does the proof come from?

Well, when Jesus met with the disciples, he breathed on them and with that, what Jesus did was fill all those with the same Holy Spirit that was within Jesus when he was on the earth. And he breathed it into the disciples. Jesus sent out the disciples in exactly the same way as he was sent by God. And for what purpose did Jesus fill his disciples? It was to live like him, to do exactly the same things as what Jesus did. To be sent just as God had sent him. To live as Christians.

No one has ever seen the Holy Spirit. He's never been able to be bottled up, to be put on display in a museum. But day in, day out, we see the effects of the Holy Spirit. He lives on within us, helping us to live every day, doing the things that God wants us to be a part of. The sceptics will dismiss that, but I believe that the wind exists. I've never ever seen the wind, but even after a big storm, I've definitely seen the full effects of the wind. In the same way, I've felt the effects of the Holy Spirit. Sometimes, we don't really focus on the Holy Spirit, because we aren't sure what he's really like. He's so busy in what he does and he does so many different things. I've been a witness to healings, I've heard the speaking of tongues, I've seen people really on fire for God – they're all different effects of the Spirit. All genuine bona-fide proof of it too. And I've felt the effects of the Holy Spirit in my life in different ways.

One time that springs to mind is when I believe the Holy Spirit prompted me to ask a girl in the youth group what she wanted praying for. We didn't do that kind of thing really and I had no idea what her problems were, but the Holy Spirit was at work within me. It makes you very humble when you realise that he's really there, a part of you. It's a privilege, don't you agree? They're just illustrations of the way that I've experienced the Holy Spirit – you may have examples and experiences too, maybe sometimes without even knowing that it was the Holy Spirit. Be brave enough to share your experience of the Holy Spirit with a close Christian friend. The second you accept Jesus into your life, you welcome the Holy Spirit. Don't be afraid of the work he does. The Holy Spirit is the legacy that Jesus left to us and is vitally important.

So, the resurrection of Jesus doesn't have to be seen in its entirety to be believed. It wasn't just a date in history; it was the beginning of a new era when Jesus gave us the Holy Spirit to continue the work that he has begun on the earth. We are so lucky to have such an empowerment, an amazing gift from God for his disciples to use to do his work.

Have you truly accepted Jesus into your life as risen Lord, and do you see him, like Thomas as your Lord and your God? If not, and you want to, do it today. Tell him how great his resurrection was and accept the Holy Spirit to be a massive and great part of your life.

To finish, I hear Elvis is alive, back from the dead, and living in Milton Keynes. I don't believe it! However, I've heard Jesus Christ is alive, back from the dead and living amongst us. That's a fact and the truth! Make sure that he's living through the Holy Spirit in you.

BACK TO BASICS
Understanding the simple things

RICH TEA & BAPTISTRY

Food has always been a big part of my life. In fact, I really like my food and will eat anything. I think that's what it is that contributes to my fluctuating waistline through life.

I am partial to a biscuit and have been munching on those supposedly 'healthy' biscuits that are good for you. I'm sure they're not, but hey, they taste good and it makes me feel good that I'm eating healthily.

I had the opportunity to link biscuits and baptism once for a service and it was a bizarre link. It was a fun way of describing Baptism and God had his way when it was revealed that there was someone in church that morning interested in getting their kids 'done'.

We are called to use more and more creative ways of sharing the gospel – after all, we follow the most amazing story teller who used all sorts of ways to get his message across. We can't always trust our fail-safe way of sharing the gospel. If we don't work on communicating in a bright and colourful way, inevitably, we will become stale. The biscuits in our house never reach that stage.

✪✪✪✪✪

RICH TEA & BAPTISTRY

Stereotyping is something that humans can't avoid. In fact, the world is full of stereotypes. Christians have some that affect them as we are stereotyped by our clothes, actions and food! How often is a comic Christian portrayed wearing sandals? I'm sure some do, but not all and a good job really, because my feet stink! What about the way we act – the guitar-playing 'trendy' vicar. Ten times out of ten will be shown playing a large acoustic guitar with a rainbow strap! Actually, there are a lot of them around! Finally, food! It doesn't matter where you go - a faith tea is guaranteed to have Quiche of some sort. Whether it's got broccoli, ham or even last Sunday's leftovers, quiche has its own place in Christian events.

However, one of the most popular foods that Christians seem to spend their yearly entertainment budget on is to buy thousands of packs of Rich Tea biscuits! The manufacturers must make an absolute fortune from selling acres of the things every year. Apologies if you like them, but they aren't that exciting! They'd make better use as coasters. However, all the coffee mornings that I've been to seem to have them. Christians do seem to enjoy buying them, and I think I've found the reason why we spend, spend, spend on these boring biscuits!

You see, they are the ultimate dunking biscuit. Hopefully, you are like me, not too posh or hygienic to have a dunk, but what I do with a Rich Tea biscuit to make it exciting is take it above my cup and then, dunk! Not for too long because there will be bits left in the bottom. However, in my analysis of biscuits, it's a practise that Rich Tea's should not do without.

All this biscuit rambling will do nothing to stop the inevitable rumbling noises that are coming from my stomach, but dunking biscuits did get me thinking. Maybe because I have a strange mind but I ended up thinking about dunking biscuits and baptism in the same way. You see, the dunking of biscuits is similar, not identical of course, but similar to what John the Baptist did to baptise people which we read about in John 1. When we take a biscuit and dunk it into a drink, whether its tea or coffee, we want to make it taste a lot better – a better flavour! Is that why we do it? I think so.

By getting the Rich Tea wet with a flavoured drink, it becomes a tastier snack and loads better! In a similar way, by Baptism, people have a different flavour to their lives. When John baptised people, he not only made them new and clean, he improved life for them. By being saved from their sins, they had a new way to go and a new exciting life to look forward to. All this by dunking them in the River Jordan! What he did was very significant. He wasn't just trying to dunk people in the water - he was cleansing them of their sins. It was a very important process and thousands flocked from miles around to witness this. Baptism was so exciting! So you see, in a way, both the Rich Tea biscuits and those baptised were getting a new flavour!

However, in the 21st Century, it makes me angry just how insignificant some people have made Baptism or the whole process of being Christened. One of the phrases that I hate to hear is when people say that they are taking the baby to be "done"! Baptism is a vital part of being a Christian. The way of saying that people are taking the baby to be "done" makes it sound as though it's like the babies having their jabs – just part of the walk of life. It's not the case for all baptisms, but there are plenty of non-church regulars that see coming to church for a baptism or a christening as getting their kids "done"!

I'm excited by the many churches today that are now offering a dedication service. Some stalwart members of the church see this kind of service as less meaningful and bad, but what is forgotten is that the offer of a dedication service is a great way to evangelise. Think about it! It may seem non-inclusive, but it's great because when folk ring up to get christened at any age, they will get challenged by having to ask themselves "Can I really keep the promises I make? Do I really want to do all those things? Can I really offer a Christian home?" It's refreshing to see people challenged like this especially when we know there are many churches and clergy about that would gladly say "A Christening? Come along and bring all of your friends! That will make the church look full!" The idea of offering an alternative to Baptism is great for those that aren't willing to keep the promises they make.

The question is, though, why is it important to be baptised? Is it just a naming ceremony or is it so much more? The constitution of the Anglican Church states that 'anyone living in the parish has the right to be baptised and the minister can only recommend, not refuse, if he feels that it shouldn't happen!" So the whole idea of Baptism is really important and for all who want to come and be baptised. After all, we have parties for a baptism, sending gifts and cards. We do get excited about it. Should we get excited about this naming ceremony or is there something a lot deeper involved?

When we are baptised, we are following a lead set by Jesus years ago. John baptised Jesus in the River Jordan. John had been baptising loads of people already – he was asking people to repent and then they'd be made clean! But he was clear when we was saying that someone more important was coming to baptise with fire, not water! He even said, in Matthew 3, verse 10, that it was someone whose "sandals that he wasn't worthy to untie!" He knew it was Jesus. And then, Jesus came to him. John realised how important Jesus was and in John 1, verse 29, John referred to Jesus as "The Lamb of God, who takes away the sin of the world". However, Jesus asked him "can you baptise me?" and reluctantly, he did baptise Jesus.

It was important for Jesus to get baptised by John. This is what Jesus needed to do to begin his ministry, and did it by being baptised in the River Jordan by John. Do you think it was just a case of a naming ceremony then for Jesus or was it a little bit more than that?

I think from what happened that it was a lot more. It doesn't happen every time we host a christening or a Baptism, but when Jesus was baptised, the Holy Spirit, shaped like a dove filled him and God proclaimed "This is my son whom I love!" Imagine how full the churches would be if every time someone is baptised, God booms out "I made this one!" Today, it doesn't happen as graphically, but it does happen.

We are giving ourselves to God and that it exactly what we should do. We must give ourselves wholly and completely in everything we do – not just on a Sunday morning, or at bible study or cell groups, but in every aspect of our lives. We need to make sure that people know we are crazy about God and God is crazy about us, as mankind.

You see that is what Baptism is about, dedicating our lives to God and giving ourselves completely to him – totally getting the "SACK". The SACK? What does that mean?

Well, Jesus had three things happen to him when he was baptised and these are the same three things that happen to us when we first give ourselves to God. Firstly, Jesus "submitted" himself to God! The process of submission is to give or offer something and in Jesus' case, himself. Although church actively encourages Baptism, it is a choice. When we are younger, we don't know it, but it is a choice to follow God and become a Christian. Jesus knew that he had to be baptised, but even for him, it was still an option – one which thankfully for us, he did say "Yes, I know that I am here for a reason. I am going to follow that path and I submit myself to do this." After wrestling with Satan in the desert and choosing to stay focused on God, he went to John and was ready for three years of ministry. Like Jesus, we have to do the same. We should be able to recognise that we need God, we need his Grace and so therefore, we have to totally submit ourselves to God and he will cleanse us through what Jesus has done.

The second thing that happened at the Baptism was that in the form of the dove, he "admitted" the Holy Spirit. Admission means to allow something entry. As we heard, the Holy Spirit was sent down and admitted into Jesus to enable him to do his ministry. It's the same for us! When we submit ourselves to God, we can expect to receive the Holy Spirit within us to fill us and enable us to do our own ministries, whatever they may be. You may be gifted in making friends, serving or leading, but the Holy Spirit helps us to do these. He doesn't necessarily come down in the shape of a dove, but the Spirit does come into us to guide us and influence us in our daily lives as with Jesus.

The third thing that happened was the commission from God. A commission comes when someone is chosen to do something. When Jesus was baptised, God's commission came in the form of God speaking out from heaven. God said "This is my son, whom I love!" – A true commissioning from

God. In the same way, God commissions us. He loves us and he speaks to us in many ways, through others, directly, or he makes the opportunities available to us. Sometimes, we may feel that we haven't had a commissioning. Maybe God didn't speak in the way that we thought – but he has commissioned us! Whatever we do, we have that commissioning from God – be it on the church council, playing the organ, painting the walls, writing to a friend, making the tea, even buying the biscuits! Sometimes, we think God is just sending out people for the things that can be greatly recognised in the world's eyes, but he wants people to offer themselves for many tasks, no matter how big or small you think it is. That is God's commissioning for you!

The final part of the SACK comes with the letter "K" which stands for Kick Start! Jesus was baptised and all this happened at the start of his ministry. It should be the same for us. By giving ourselves to God, being filled with the Holy Spirit and then going on a journey with God, that's the start of life for Christians. By doing this, we can Kick Start our new life. Maybe for some of us, it could mean we need to start again! But at baptism, all this culminates in the Kick Start.

That's the SACK.

Our **S**ubmission
Our **A**dmission
Our **C**ommission
Our **K**ick Start

That's what our baptism should be.

We need to constantly be doing all of these – reminding ourselves that we submitted to God, continue to ask God to send his Holy Spirit to be within us and carrying out God's calling. That should be what our Christian life is all about, not just what happens on the day that we become a Christian, or when we are baptised – it's our Christian life and our Christian mission.

Yes, a mission! Our Christian path and walk with God is a mission that we have been called for and we can see that in the things that we have looked at. We begin with our Submission to God, then the Admission of the Holy Spirit and finally, our Commission from God. These three give us the basis for our Christian life. It helps us get excited about being a Christian – we are on a mission! Now, we don't need to get out our James Bond-style clothing and pretend that we are a secret spy, but we, as a church, are on a God-sent mission and surely we can get excited about that!

I know that being a Christian doesn't seem that exciting – but it is! We have a God who is so amazing, he created the whole world. We just need to look around us to realise that! We have a Saviour, Jesus, who in his life was so revolutionary that he changed the whole world forever, and even died for each one of us so that we can get to heaven. We have the Holy Spirit that comes within us to aid us so much through life and do amazing things within us. Isn't that exciting? We need to get excited about these things!

However, we aren't that excited. Not necessarily as individuals with our personalities, or what our social life is like, but with our faith and as a church, we're not that excited! After all, church isn't the most excited place to be – what with the meetings we have, and sometimes, the services. Church should be an exciting place to be. It should be full of people who are not just excited about how many goals were scored by their team on Saturday, or the new TV that's now the centrepiece of the living room, but also, animated and excited about our relationship with Jesus and the faith that we have! I don't mean to put it in a silly way, but in my eyes, it seems to me that too many Christians are Rich Tea biscuits – in need of a bit of a dunking in the Holy Spirit to make them more excited about their faith. Imagine the difference in reaction when offered a Jaffa Cake, Jammie Dodgers or a Hob Nob, my favourite biscuit. They are loads more appealing and people really want to eat them because they have something going on, with oats, with Jam or with Orange. So much more interesting! We need to be like them – exciting, but so exciting and full of our faith that people cannot fail to be interested when we share the gospel with them.

So, I'll conclude as I began – with biscuits! Don't forget, we are on a mission and one that God has got mapped out for us. To help us on the way, let's not forget that Jesus was baptised and what that baptism means for us. And we need to keep on submitting to God, admitting the Holy Spirit and following God's commission and by doing that, kick-starting an exciting mission with God. Let's be excited and exciting – let's not be the one biscuit in the tin that people don't want to touch, but let's be the one that people want to pick first – the ones that bring a smile to the face. Be excited about being a Christian and people will become excited! Let's be a place full of excitement. If we want the church to grow, you know what we have to do! Fill the place with Jammie Dodgers like me and you!

HOUSE FIRE

I'm scared of getting burnt, mainly because I know it hurts! Something to do with pouring hot oil over my hands whilst cooking prawn crackers! It let me with a pretty nasty scar that I'm sure will never go away and it will always remind me of the time cooking oil and I had a closer relationship. Or maybe my fear comes from sitting in the front seat of the car and taking the cigarette lighter out to see if it was really hot to handle. I also did a similar experiment with an iron!

Yet, the Holy Spirit comes as tongues of fire and burns inside of us. Yep, as a Christian, I'm desperate to be burnt by God's Spirit and hopefully, touching others too. I suppose we are like cattle and have been branded with the Holy Spirit, showing God's mark quite clearly!

Now that's a scar that I don't mind showing off! The reading shows how it all began

✪✪✪✪✪

HOUSE FIRE

It was Pentecost and we were all gathered together, hiding ourselves away down in someone's upstairs room in case we got beat up – it was incredibly likely that would happen! Goodness knows what we were talking about, but we were discussing what to do. You'd never guess what happened next. It was just so strange...

Suddenly, there was a great wind that came into the whole house – incredible! The wind swept across the room and almost knocked us off our chairs! All the doors were shut and we couldn't work it out, but it was like a wind coming from heaven, blowing us, but refreshing us.

Then, something like tongues of fire came down, but not just setting fire to the room. They seemed to touch each one of us – we were awash with this fire and it didn't burn us, it filled us! Suddenly, out of nowhere, a sound of languages unheard before – languages from all over the world – what a noise! People were shouting out and filled with extra power! It was something totally unusual, totally unorthodox – supernatural!

We ventured outside and into the world to meet a bunch of people all wondering what on earth was going on. People could understand the different languages being said! People from different countries, different regions were seeing these people talk in their native tongue. They were confused and started shouting – "They are talking of the great things God has done, but they're Galileans! It's not possible!" The cynics shouted "Disgrace! They're drunk! These people are foolish!"

Then all stopped and Peter spoke up. "Listen up people! They're not drunk! It's 9am! But you are witness to something very special! Let me ask you a question – do you believe in the Supernatural?"

TAKE A DEEP BREATH

I often want to talk of how great it is to know the Holy Spirit and rejoice having Him on your side. It is refreshing to get help at times.

I took the following message to a church and never fully delivered it, because half-way through, God had other ideas. He wanted something different to happen and I suppose the biggest compliment you can give when explaining the Holy Spirit to people is at times, he is inexplicable! That's what makes it really exciting! It's beyond rationality and totally supernatural.

✪✪✪✪✪

TAKE A DEEP BREATH

Imagine being holed up in a room with nowhere to go – afraid to leave in case someone will pretty much beat you up. Not really knowing the future or totally understanding the past, if you'd have been a disciple, things would have taken a big u-turn. The man that you'd followed for the last three years, you'd seen to talk to just days after you'd seen him killed on a cross. Then, quite literally, you'd seen him disappear into the clouds. What on earth was going to happen? That's what it was like to be part of the very first church and to be one of the first disciples.

Then Pentecost came and changed the world forever. Pentecost was a festival full of celebration amongst the Jews and still is! They were celebrating the harvest of the wheat and spent their time eating, drinking and listening to music. Pretty much something that sounds fun! You could say that, but the disciples couldn't take part in fear of persecution – they were shut away hidden from the world!

Then God decided that they should be out there, making a difference. He sent the Holy Spirit in strong wind and touching them with tongues of fire.

What do you reckon it would have been like? Sitting in a room minding your own business and then tongues of fire licking away at your head and filling you with a power that you know nothing about! And then, you found yourself speaking a language that you'd never heard before. It would be something truly supernatural! Something that's incomprehensible – we can't really gauge what it was like! It's something we can't quite understand.

It must have been confusing for them at the time and that's where the cynics could come in and say "Ah, they're drunk!"

The irony is that they were drunk, but not in the way that the critics thought! You see, they were under the influence of something very powerful, more powerful than any drink they could have had. They had the Holy Spirit within them, causing them to act in a strange way that they were not used to.

When Peter spoke afterwards, he was direct and exclaimed the truth of what was happening. After Jesus had ascended into heaven, the Holy Spirit would come. Jesus even promised this in John 7 when he says "If anyone thirsts, let him come to me and drink. Rivers of living water will brim and spill out of the depths of anyone who believes in me this way, just as the Scripture says." This is what he was talking about – this happening at Pentecost! But when Peter spoke, three thousand were baptised and were eager to receive the Holy Spirit. They called out and they received.

You know what? Christmas is an exciting time of year – you get presents and have parties! What about Easter? It's the most important time in the church calendar and you get loads of chocolate eggs to eat! Don't you enjoy Easter?

For me, the most exciting time of the year is Pentecost. It's because it signifies something very special for Christians. It's the time of the year when we realise that we are not alone! It's something that really excites me, because we have something that no-one else lays claim to. Magicians have tricks – making you genuinely believe that they can saw someone in half. You can read your stars in the paper that the writers generalise things so much that they could apply to anyone. We, as Christians, have something that is truly supernatural that we struggle to explain – a sort of extraordinary ability and power that's within us. It is one of the things that I am genuinely excited about being a Christian – after all, church isn't that exciting and the Bible is a tough read at times, but the Holy Spirit is very real, very active today and so vital! Christians need Him, as much as air or food!

You see, the Holy Spirit coming wasn't just a historical happening for Pentecost; it was the start of things to come and a new beginning for the church. The Holy Spirit came to be part of the people of God's lives.

It's a simple concept really – do you play tennis? Playing tennis is really easy if you have the right tools to play with – try playing it without a ball! Pretty confusing I guess.

It's the same for Christians – you can't talk the talk or walk the walk without this power inside you. You meet a genuine bona-fide Christian, not a church-goer, but someone with the Holy Spirit within them and they are awash in the fruits of the Spirit – loving, joyful, peaceful, patient, kind, good, faithful, gentle and calm. He doesn't make us those things, but he helps us achieve them. We are filled with God's amazing fruit juice to use in life.

Let's never forget that at Pentecost, God filled us up to make a difference in the world. Let's rely on the Holy Spirit to govern our lives!

CHANGING YOUR ANGLE
A different way of looking at things

YOU CAN'T PLEASE EVERONE CAN YOU?

Is the Bible relevant?

It's a question that Christians are encouraged to always answer "Yes" to! Of course it is. You are wrongly told that if you think otherwise, you should be cast away from the church. How dare we think otherwise that the Bible isn't relevant?

The truth is that the Bible is always relevant and the message means as much today as it did two thousand years ago. I don't doubt that! But the way that we need to present the Bible is constantly changing! We need to keep ahead of ourselves, always looking at ways of presenting the Bible stories in active ways. Books like Eugene Petersen's "The Message" and Nick Page's "Bible Book" are great presentations of the Gospel.

Sometimes, we don't do that so well. I've been at churches before where the readings have been read in a monotonous way from the King James Bible. Of course, the long-standing church members loved it, but the looks of bewilderment from the younger members of the church meant that the reading, no matter how good the content, went whooshing over their heads. They were unable to grasp things beyond the "thee's" and "thou's".

Each church is, of course, different, but in order to grow, we need to be actively making the truth relevant. The message should never change. I consider the late Rob Lacey as something of a hero for his interpretation of the "Street Bible", an amazing resource for the church. It brings the word of God accessible for a section of society that needs good news.

Unfortunately, though, we do get a divide between those that seek to worship in a traditional way and those that want to worship in a more modern way. Many churches have split because of such a thing! I hope the following reading goes someway to meeting the needs of both extremes!!

YOU CAN'T PLEASE EVERYONE, CAN YOU?

When the folks had seeneth that Jesus and all his fans had doneth a complete vanishing act, they jumped on the nearest ferries, in facteth, right in front of them, and raced off to Capernaum in pursuiteth of Jesus and his crew.

They seeketh him here, they seeketh him there, they seeketh him absolutely everywhere. Eventually, the merry crowd of people found him on the other side of the laketh. Rather annoyed, but relieved to find him, they relaxedeth and said "Oi Jesus, why on eartheth did you come here? We were lookingeth for you for donkey's years!"

Jesus looked quizzically, as he did, and said "Right, listeneth all you lot, and listeneth good! I ain't gonna lie to you now. You haven't cometh searching for me cos I did a miracleth have you? Oh no, I'd put my reputation on the lineth to say that to you that you haveth come because you ate the breadeth and are feeling stuffedeth and fed well! Am I righteth?" Jesus was in full floweth now and didn't hangeth about for an answer. "Listeneth to me, clotheth ears, don't keep working and buy foodeth that is going to go stinkyeth and mouldyeth and greeneth, you've got to keep working towards getting the foodeth that will always be good!"

A person piped up from the crowdeth. "Jesus, where can I get this foodeth? The last time I was in Sainsbury'seth, they didn't seemeth to have it on special offer! Will they stocketh it if I asketh?"

Jesus tutted to himself and muttered "what a fooleth!" He then spoke aloud "You can only get this foodeth via the Son of Man, because God had made sure he has enough power in Him!"

The voice piped up. "Cooleth! Does he have a websiteth?"

"No" Jesus said.

"Faxeth?" replied the man.

"Don't be daft" Jesus replied, getting agitated.

"Can I have his mobileth numbereth then?" The man enquired.

"See that laketh behind you" said Jesus, frustrated. "I walked on it! Can you walketh under it?"

A different person shouted "Jesus. I have a questioneth. A real one! Erm, what exactly does God want us to do? Telleth us!"

Jesus said "Ah-haeth!" It was the question he'd been waiting for. "Right, this is what work you have got to do for God as your guvnoreth. Just believe everything the One he sent tells you! Just listeneth to me and believe basically!"

"Oh, OKeth", said one. "Believe you? Are you the one he sent?"

Jesus frowned. "I am that. God sent me!"

"Mmmeth" said the man. "I'm not sure! Could you just do us guys a favoureth, please?"

"What is that?" Jesus replied, surprised.

The man was confident. "Well, u see, can you do a miracleth to prove that you are the Son of Man? If we get to see you do something micarulouseth, then we'll believe you, we promise! You know Moses, old guy, lived a long time ago. Well, he ate Manna in the desert and he madeth the manna raineth down from the skies onto the people. I know cos it says so in the Old Testament!"

Jesus muttered to himself. "I've just walked on water and fed five thousand families with scraps of foodeth! These people! No wonder they need saving!" He then stood and shouted with force "You just don't get it, do you! Right, listeneth up and listeneth doubly good, I shall say this only once! Moses didn't raineth manna down from above, God did! Do you getteth that? It was God that sends the true bread from heaven! God's bread comes down and makes sureth everyone can liveth full lives!"

A familiar voice comes up from the crowd. "Do you know who makes this? Is it Hoviseth? Or Warbutonseth? And is it thicket or thineth slices? I could really do with that bread!"

Jesus sighed and replied "The Bread is in the form of the one he sent, not sliced!"

"To be fair, Jesus, you don't looketh like a loaf of bread. Can you be toasted?"

"No, just sunburneth", Jesus exclaimed!

"Very funny, I don't think, and anyway, we can't buttereth you or eateth you!"

"No, of course not! Why does there haveth to be one?" Jesus winced.

The man continued, "So, we can't eateth you, buttereth you or toasteth you! In what way do you represent bread, then?"

Jesus steadied himself. "You don't need to take it literally, I am speaking spiritually! Listeneth to this, cos someone may writeth a hymn about it one day! And you can say I was there!" He paused. "I AM THE BREAD OF LIFE! I will feed you spiritually so that you can lead a full life. I will make sure your spirit is full and you can come to God. Get it? Basically, for those who follow me, they will never be hungry and if you take the time to believe in me, you'll never be thirsty. Have I explained myself? Do you get me?"

A big cheereth went up from the crowd. Shouts and proclamations went up! "Yes, Lord, give useth the bread always! We wanteth to follow you!"

Jesus sighed a satisfied sigh. "Finally! You understand me!"

"Yeseth, we believeth in Youeth, Jesuseth!"

"Thanks" said Jesus to himself. "This preaching lark is pretty hard, you know!" He then addressed the crowd. "Thanks for understanding. You guys, you'll be the death of me you know."

LOVE IS...

Your wedding day! The happiest day of your life! Months, sometimes, years have gone into planning the festivities for your nearest and dearest. But at the end of the day, it's worth it!

Weddings have lots in them these days. It's become a time when you have to "keep up with the Jones". Weddings cost an absolute fortune (you should take your bank manager if you go to a wedding fayre!) A traditional wedding has to have a punch-up with two family members that don't get on, someone being drunk, and some clever joker trying to cough during the service when the minister asks for any objections. A stressful day! The happiest day of your life – "don't make me laugh" some say!

But not me! Our wedding day was a great day and exciting. It was great to get together so many friends and family and to celebrate. But what was also exciting is that with many non-Christians in the room, we were able to declare that we needed God as part of our marriage and we still do! It was exciting to have the opportunity to give the day to God!

One thing that is very common though is the very famous reading from 1 Corinthians 13. Paul never wrote it for the reason that it is now used in describing two people uniting, it was about the importance of following God and loving him. In that relationship, nothing's more important than love! The reading below gives it a different twist!

✪✪✪✪✪

LOVE IS...

If I talk the talk and say the right things, but do not say it with love, then it's just insignificant noise! If I can predict the future, have heavenly knowledge and can do the impossible, but forget what part love plays, then I am worthless. If I give up everything I've got and put my life on the line, but do it without love, I might as well not bother.

What is love? Love patiently waits, love compassionately care. Love isn't wary; love is not disrespectful, love isn't self-centred. Love doesn't get easily irritated, instead love forgives and forgets. Love doesn't always applaud evil but smiles on goodness. Love always defends, always believes, always aspires and is in for the long haul. Love never disappoints.

Predictions will stop, tongues will quieten and wisdom will fail. Our wisdom and predicting are for now, but when perfection comes, anything that is imperfect will disappear. I was young once and I acted my age. My words were simple, my mind was imaginative, what I knew was uncomplicated. As a man, I acted like a man leaving my old ways behind.

I can only cope with so much now, but at the end of time, I'll see God face to face. I know I'm not perfect now, but on that day, I'll know perfection through God and God will know me.

So what have we got left to live with? Just a faith in God, a hope for the future and the love that he sends. But of all of these, nothing's more important than love.

CHILD PROPHECY

Who was this guy? John the Baptist – bet you can guess what he was good at!

If you were to put John in the world today, I think he would get quite a strange welcome. He was a touch unorthodox in what he wore, what he ate and how he acted. Yet, he was proud of his individuality!

He did prepare the way for Jesus and for that, he deserves great recognition. As for the rest of his life, let's see what the goggle-box would make of him.

✪✪✪✪✪

CHILD PROPHECY

Drama featuring a Presenter (Pres) and John the Baptist (John)

Pres: Well, it's often a wonder as to what it would be like to be present 2000 years ago and to really know what was going on. However, completely at your expense, we have managed to get a very, very special guest here, all the way from the first century, to tell us a bit about life in those times. He smelt a lot, so we've cleaned him up and leant him some clothes, so I'd like to make him feel very welcome and give a massive round of applause as we meet... John the Baptist!

(Applause as John enters the stage)

Pres: It's an absolute pleasure to meet you, John.
John: (nods very slowly) Pickled Gherkin.
Pres: Yes right whatever. Anyway, we have bought you here hoping that you would be able to share some wisdom with us.

John: Share some experience. Me, myself and I can do some share. Share. Cher. Hey, Sonny and Cher. Remember them. I got you, Babe. Good old Cher. Mind you, never looks any older. Must be plastic surgery. She's got more plastic than Barclaycard.
Pres: Stop John. We are not talking about Sonny and Cher.
John: Oh, shares as in stocks and shares. Arcadia went up, Consignia went down. The FTSE closes at 2 points down. How does that compare against the Dow Jones?
Pres: No. Not stocks and shares either.
John: Oh. Tables and Shares. Or Armshares.
Pres: JOHN! All I want you to do is tell us a little bit about your life and answer some very, very simple questions. Is there any chance you can do that? Can you just answer some QUESTIONS?
John: (pause) Christians? Followers of Jesus Christ...
Pres: QUESTIONS! I WANT YOU TO ANSWER SOME QUESTIONS!
John: OK. Questions. I get you. There's no need to shout.
Pres: Right. (Breathes heavily) Can you do that?
John: Yes, I think so.
Pres: Good. Now that we've done a little bit of research on you – looking through it, I'm not sure it's all correct; someone has made it up, cos it's too silly, but we've sacked her. Anyway, here we go!
John: OK.
Pres: Right. Born approximately 3 months BC in Judea, to your parents Zechariah and Elizabeth, both close to drawing their pension and both say that your birth was foretold to them by angels. Is this correct?
John: Every word of it. 100% correct.
Pres: I see. Were they OK? All there in the head, like?
John: My dad was a respected priest and my mum was also a well-respected lady. Of course they were OK!
Pres: OK. My next question is one that has surely been written down wrong. These researchers, eh? Can't get the staff! How old were you when you spoke your first words?
John: Now, let me see (counts on hands) approximately eight days old.

Pres: EIGHT DAYS? Not eight months.
John: Nope – one week and one day old.
Pres: And that doesn't strike you as a little strange?
John: No. Why should it?
Pres: Well, it usually takes about eight months! What did you say? Mama or Dada? Which one?
John: Well, I just started praising really. Various scriptures from Isaiah – all sorts of different praises to God.
Pres: At eight days old? How strange!
John: Not really. I was filled with the Spirit.
Pres: Oh I see. You were given lots of "the spirit" as a baby. That may explain your parents too. What spirit was it exactly?
John: I was filled with the Holy Spirit – direct from God.
Pres: At eight days old! This is getting very strange. Let's move on. What was school like for you?
John: Well, I continued praised God and well, at school, the other kids they used to laugh and call me names and wouldn't let me join in any of their games. I just kept on praising and telling them that they'd love me with glee and that I'd go down in history.
Pres: But they took the Mickey out of you?
John: Yeah, they did.
Pres: Funny that! Can't begin to imagine why they would. So what happened next? You grew up. I read that you were voted as Hello Magazine's Worst-dressed male of zero29. Why is that?
John: I have no idea. I just went into the desert and made a dress out of camel's hair and held it up with a leather belt.
Pres: You wore a camel hair dress.
John: Yeah.
Pres: You don't really care what other people think, do you?
John: No, not really.
Pres: Good job. Anyway, you say you were in the desert. How did you manage for food?
John: I ate honey.
Pres: Aww, that's quite normal really. I like honey. Honey's pretty normal.

John: Yeah, I like honey too. I used to spread it on wild locusts.
Pres: And ate it?
John: Yes. I ate wild locusts with honey all the time.
Pres: Yuk! I think I'm going to be sick. Weren't you? You are very strange you know!
John: Thanks.
Pres: So what did you do in the desert apart from eating live insects and build sandcastles?
John: I preached.
Pres: (laughs) and I suppose you had a good audience. What did you do? Covert millions of grains of sand?
John: No. Lots of people came from all over the land to listen to me preach. I had a word from God that I could baptise people again and wash their sin away.
Pres: So, you baptised people? Of course you did. You're John the Baptist, Baptism is your trademark. How did you do that?
John: Well, I got them in the water and sort of pushed them under and held them there so that their sins were forgiven.
Pres: Didn't you get arrested for attempting to drown people?
John: No, of course not. I was sent from God.
Pres: Yeah, yeah. So you say. Did you baptise anyone famous?
John: I baptised my cousin. He was quite famous.
Pres: What was his name?
John: Jesus. It was quite an experience that day.
Pres: Whoa, wait a minute, stop a second. Are you saying that you got Jesus Christ, our Saviour, the Son of Man, the Prince of Peace, you managed to get him baptised. You must have paid him a lot for that sort of publicity?
John: Well, actually, he came to me to be baptised. I never went out looking for him.
Pres: Sorry, he came to you to be baptised?
John: Yes, he did. It was a great day. I baptised him and then God spoke and told him that he was his Son and he loved him. And then the Holy Spirit filled him. It was a great day. My call from God was fulfilled.

Pres: So, you baptised Jesus? I can't get hold of this. Can I ask you something?

John: Fire away.

Pres: No disrespect meant, but your parents were a bit odd, you were an odd man of nature who has been preaching since he was 8 days old, you live in the desert, you wear camel skin, you eat locusts and you try and drown people to cleanse them of their sins. Fair's fair – you are completely insane and a total nutcase.

John: So you say.

Pres: And yet, despite your obvious insanity, Jesus, God's own Son, decided to choose you to purify him and cleanse him for his work on earth?

John: I suppose he did, yeah.

Pres: And God chose you to prepare the way?

John: Yes, he did.

Pres: This is a bit much for me to take in. Thanks for being interviewed, John, but I can take no more. I can't deal with any more strange revelations. John the Baptist, everyone.

John: OK. Good bye.

(John leaves and goes and sits down)

Pres: What a nutcase! Locusts, Camel Hair, Dunking, Jesus. That confirms it then – Jesus really does go and meet anyone – people as strange as John the Baptist! If God can use nutcases like him to change the world, then he can use every single one of us. Jesus' coming is truly for all.

(Presenter leaves the studio)

GET INTO GEAR
Moving in the right direction

DO AS I SAY!

Isn't it funny how so many people are good at talking the talk and can never walk the walk? I'm a football fan and have stood on the terraces for many years trying to tell the weary lads on the pitch exactly how they could be a better team. It's a good job they've never seen me play, because they would see that I can tell them how to play, but couldn't demonstrate it – hypocrite!

So often, we have great ideas about what we should do with our lives and then let ourselves down. We preach on not worrying and spend all week worrying about how the talk will go. We talk about how we will save the lost and then worry when a new face arrives in church. We pray for the forgiveness of sins and then turn around and sin again.

Fortunately, we can have a relationship with God who does want to make it all right with us again. When we stumble, he helps us bounce back up again. When we fail to do what we say we should be doing, he's there for us again.

Let's make sure that we walk and talk at the same time.

✪✪✪✪✪

DO AS I SAY!

Have you ever met someone that you could look up to in faith? Religious and evangelistic, known for awesome meetings, dedicated prayer and seen to be doing acts of kindness. Sounds good? A person that was well aware of the scriptures, part of a large, well-respected radical movement and someone you could describe as spiritual. Sound like a great Christian?

Actually, I've actually just described a Pharisee!

It's scary, isn't it? It bears an uncomfortable resemblance to many of today's churches. However, scarier is that a movement that sounds a bit like what we are aiming for is what many sermons pick up on and aggressively lay into to back up Jesus' teaching.

For the Pharisees, the Sermon on the Mount as we hear in Matthew 5 must have gone down like a lead balloon. Seeing all of the sinners around them and expecting Jesus to say well done, be more like them, imagine their horror when Jesus said things like "The First shall be last" and "the meek will inherit." To be completely honest, Jesus had it in for the Pharisees and he didn't for the sinners. He hated the public displays of faith and many a time, was a huge critic of the way the Pharisees were living.

Let's be completely honest – Jesus said that the Pharisees were hypocrites. He was right, they were! They decided to pick on other people rather than examine their own faults. In fact, a great case of spending their time picking the specks of dust they could see in other people's eyes and not picking out the logs in their own.

Hypocrisy is still a big part of church today! How often do we see it? Let's not mix what we do on a Sunday morning with the rest of our life. I know that we often decide that some places are not the place for talking about God. It's a long honoured tradition that the two things you never discuss in social conversation are politics and religion. Well, if God and Jesus mean as much to people as they make out, then anywhere is the place.

Have you put yourself in danger of being a hypocrite?

I think anyone who claims not to have ever been a hypocrite is lying. We all have, at some point. It's a phrase said "that the biggest cause of atheism in the world today is Christians who speak out through their mouths and are then let down buy their lifestyle". True. We all mess up and if we don't, then why do we need Jesus to have died for us. That isn't an invitation to go wrong, because then I really doubt whether you are sorry for what you do. God knows you inside out and will know when you are really confessing or just saying so because it feels like the right thing to do.

Think before you speak. Time and time again, we look around, like our friends the Pharisees and say "Hmm, they are not living as they should be." It's so, so wrong of us. Jesus never criticised the sinners without showing them love first. We should do the same.

It would have been so easy to look at hypocrisy and look at people and think to myself "he's a hypocrite", "she's a hypocrite", but that's not my place. It's in your hearts to see. If I did decide to call people hypocrites, then I too would earn that title. I am a hypocrite sometimes! I don't do enough to make Jesus' name big. I don't always say things that I like to hear myself saying. I'm guilty of a multitude of sins on a daily basis. I'm a bit mixed-up. Even my motives are wrong sometimes. But, and a big but, God knows that, because I tell him. And he has given me some gifts too to look after here in the world. Not because I'm worthy, but because he wants me to have them.

So, my challenge is not to look for the faults in others. Look at our own. Make a conscious decision to show those you think aren't going right just what God means to you and that you can love them as a friend. That's the most important thing.

EXCUSE ME!

"I don't want to!" It's a phrase we hear far too often. "I would wash the dishes, but not this Friday!" "Of course I'd help at the summer fayre, but only after 6pm! It's finished then? Oh well!" "I'm washing my hair!"

Excuses, excuses! It makes us feel like we are justifying things when we're not really. We pretend that by being busy doing one thing, that's a good reason why we can't do the next thing. Isn't it just a case of building barriers?

We can do the same with God! We make excuses to him. I know that I tell God that I'm not ready for certain things, that it's not my turn or that I haven't got time. Deep down, I feel that I've given a good answer!

Trust God, then, to prove me wrong! Even when you try and turn Him down, God says "You reckon that you can't help me out! No excuse!"

Better forget my excuses and get on with it then! Or does my hair need washing...

✪✪✪✪✪

EXCUSE ME!

I decided that I would like to go into business one day. After all, a lot of people in this country are making money and a lot of it! The best thing for me to do to catch up would be to go into business. I think that I went about it the wrong way because I decided that I'd start a trade without actually knowing what I was going to do! Probably not the wisest way, but still, I'd do it! So I looked at what I could do in Britain to make a shed load of cash! It needed to be something that British people are obsessed with!

I thought about opening a fish and chip shop! That would be so popular with the British! Then I got thinking – we aren't very much a nation that has fish and chips as its national meal anymore. We'd either order something Italian like pizza or the ever-popular Indian Curry – we find that they've become our national dishes! In fact, on a personal note, I was entertaining some Americans and they needed to have something to eat. We all went out for something traditionally English – which meant that we hit a fast food place on a Saturday night and bought Kebabs! So normal - traditional as an English snack, yet originally from Greece and Turkey! So, a fish and chip shop wasn't probably the best business to start in!

So I thought maybe why not do something about the weather – maybe a weekly magazine forecasting? British people are obsessed with the weather! It's incredible. I'm surprised that the nightly forecasts aren't number one in the ratings. I'm sure, if you're like my family, you're on first name terms with all the weather presenters! It's often you can hear the sound of "Tut! You're not sending us rain again, are you Charlie?" People are mad about it even though it's not going to change if you know or not! If I started business with a weather magazine, most people would be able to get forecasts free on the telly anyway! Ah well!

Then it struck me – the best area to get into! What do the people of this country do more than watch the weather? I needed to get into the shampoo market! That was it! Hair care was the way forward. How often do you hear someone say that they are washing their hair? All the time! That must mean that there's a fortune to be made out of shampoo – to cater for the millions that need daily attention for the nest on their head!

I'm not actually going to be in business, trying to rival the leading brands, because I'd be losing out! You see, I don't believe that people in this country are obsessed with washing their hair! I believe that people do wash their hair – good job really, otherwise we'd be a bunch of scarecrows with wiry, dirty hair! But people do often say that they are washing their hair and the reason for that is to make an excuse! And it's not that we've become a band of people really good at washing their hair, we've become a race that's good at making excuses! Think about the excuses you've made! Maybe you didn't want to go and see someone because you didn't feel like it or that you didn't want to write that letter today – I'm sure you made an excuse not to do it! We've got too good at making excuses!

The trouble is that our excuse making has filtered into the life of church and our own personal faith! We all make excuses about not doing things that we don't fancy at church – it could be your turn to do the various chores! I know that once I missed a rehearsal for a play a few years ago when I'd got supposed work to do, but that work seemed to involve watching a bit of football on the telly! I'm allowed to talk about making excuses, because I'm experienced in that department! I know a few people that when it comes to their turn to do things, suddenly there is a severe cold developed or if heavy lifting is involved, that back twinge has instantly become a problem again! I'm such a cynic, but it's true – people will make excuses so they don't have to muck in and rather more worryingly, Christians are good at making excuses!

Jesus had to encounter a few people who just wanted to make excuses when he'd decided to send out the seventy-two! This was a gang who were to go ahead of Jesus and we find further on the works that they have done in Luke 10 when demons were cast out by them in Jesus' name. Of course, you'd think that they would be a mighty, holy force – religious, spiritual men who would digest pages of scripture at three in the morning! What comes across in the Bible is that they are a bit of a wet troop! Jesus had gathered them to go on an amazing mission but scary and demanding mission. When they realised this, it wouldn't sound that fun! This was when Jesus wanted to make it clear that this was going to be really tough and they had to fully commit themselves! The first one would have nonchalantly declared smugly that "I'm good! I'll follow you anyway!" Imagine the deflation when Jesus said "We'll be sleeping rough!" Doesn't really sell it! Then the next said "I'll come, but I want funeral leave first!" Jesus was harsh and replied "He's dead! Forget him! Get on with my will!" I wonder how that would go down today! When people die, we like to say farewells, but Jesus was right when he was saying "the dead have a sealed fate – what about the living that haven't?" We might need to learn from that! The final one said "I got to have a fond farewell with my family!" Jesus was really tough again and said "We're going forward! Forget them too!" Although these men made excuses, we'd think today that they'd not be that unreasonable! If we were going on a mission, even today, we'd make adequate arrangements for sleeping, we'd give people compassionate leave, especially if it was for a parent and we'd make sure we said our goodbyes! However, when Jesus sent out the seventy-two, it really was a tough mission and whatever the excuse, it wasn't any good!

Do we do the same today? Do we make excuses to Jesus? I think sadly we do! As Christians, we've very often got an excuse for the things maybe we're called to do! It's fair to say that we will even make an excuse when God calls us! Sometimes, we'll sit there in a service and we'll be thinking at the sermon – "that's a message for someone else!" But one day, it may be for you! Sadly, we do make excuses as a church! How often have you heard Christians moaning about the fact that they can't do something? Maybe you've made the same mistake as me and tried to tell God that really you are too busy – there's not a space in your calendar? Trust me – God makes sure there is a space! Or maybe, and it's so sad to hear this one, you've had the excuse that I'm too old to do that sort of thing – I've done my bit! Trouble is, God never stops using his followers from the very young to the very old! Maybe you've used the excuse of "ah well, that's life!" It saddens me every time the church looks at its members and says that numbers are dwindling – but it's just a fact of life – Sunday's are busy! It's up to the church to do something to stop the rot!

We are excuse-makers and specialists, but when Jesus sent out the seventy-two, he didn't shirk away from the fact that it is tough. He doesn't have much time for those that want to give another reason for not going. He wants to have followers that are focused on doing his work – with no excuses.

When Jesus was telling his followers that things were hard and that there were no excuses, it was because he wanted them to be 100% into the mission, fully concentrating on taking the Kingdom of God to the world. To be truly and wholly giving their all.

That's not changed today. We are still called to be giving our all as Christians, to be continuing on the path that he's set out all through life – to be strong in faith, obedient in life and focused on what we are aiming for. Eternity with our Saviour!

Paul said in Romans 12 that he wanted the church to live as living sacrifices, holy and pleasing to God! The Romans were conforming to the way of the world, but he didn't want them to do that – he urged them to submit fully to the way that God wanted them to be and to be focused on God's will! That message is just as relevant for the 21st Century church – we still need to live a life that's pleasing to God. We don't need to conform to the way that the world's going – we need to Christ-like – truly Christian!

I think the church is focused, but I'm saddened because I'm not sure we are focused on the right things! We tend to be really concentrated on the way we go about things. We care about what people do or the way that they do them – especially if it's not a way that we like things done! Some Christians are focused on the fact that their worship service must be approximately one hour long with five hymns – some Christians are focused on the fact that we haven't got the latest gossip on Mrs Smith and we don't know what she's been up to! Some Christians are focused on petty issues – whether homosexuals should be in church, whether unmarried couples should live together, whether we should drink – I'm not supporting or condemning any of those issues, but why are focused on those sort of things? Are they not just excuses that make burying a relative or being with a family look like a major world disaster?

As a church, we need to focus not on what is wrong with our particular church – not on what irks us or offends us? After all, our focus in the church should be on the Gospel that Jesus shared. We've got it all spelt out in sixty-six books printed in black and white – now in our own language too and we need to be sharing that. We need to be proclaiming the Kingdom of God all throughout the world in every stage of our life!

We do need to be focused, but we need to be focused on God! We don't need to focus on the things that make us religious – after all, Jesus made it quite clear what he thought of the religious types! He treated the Pharisees in a way that belittled them! We need to be focused on three things – loving God, following Jesus and letting the Holy Spirit reign in our lives! And we don't need to just be focused – we need to give our all – we need to give ourselves totally!

Ask yourself a question – where do you stand? What is your relationship with God like? Do you follow Jesus as Lord and Saviour? We need to be asking that question in our hearts – if Jesus came and said "Come on, we're going on a mission – follow me", what would your reaction be? Would you want to say your goodbyes? I don't know about you but I'd hate to be the last one sitting there! I think that we have to evaluate where we stand with God – and sadly have to ask, are we saved? Some of us need to forget that church isn't a social club that we've been coming to for years – it isn't that important, no matter how impressive the building is. It's the relationship we have with God that matters.

We need to be that committed, that focused and ready at the call of God to give up everything just to follow him. Would you be able to do that – would you be able to give it all up for God just like that? It would be hard.

It's a tough call to do something like that – but no secrets have been made – the life of a Christian is tough! God made it a lot easier by sending a brilliant free gift of the Holy Spirit that we need to be able to let in. The Holy Spirit is the only one that can help us to be totally focused and committed Christians. Are we a Spirit-led church?

We should be, but you see, the Holy Spirit is a problem to a church that wants to feel comfortable, a challenge to a church that wants to keep itself to itself, a nuisance to a church that wants to go about being a church that wants to make excuses. You see, the Holy Spirit is available to all and by becoming a Christian we are able to let him in. We just open up our hearts and it feels like God is there. You have a sense of power – you know that God is within you! However, excuses don't work with God when he's provided his Spirit. God's got a plan for each one of us, you see, and he calls us whenever and wherever to do his work and his will. He calls us in many ways – directly, but also, in your minds, in the pages of a book, through the words of a friend – there's no consistency to God's calling, but he calls you and to do ALL his work! It may be that your call is one of making friends with people, or God wants you to be able to serve others through the making of tea. It could also be more extreme and he could want you to work in Africa or set up a homeless shelter. He may even want you to speak his word to others! Each one of us has a plan – but we may have the excuse. You might say – "Sorry God, I can't do that. I'm eighty-five! It's too late for me! Impossible!" God will come back and say "Remember the Holy Spirit I gave you. Nothing is impossible!"

So, I want to challenge you – whatever God is calling you to do, do it! No matter how unable you feel you are, no matter how busy you think you are, God will be with you, so go for it! And live your life by giving yourself wholly to him – don't forget that on a wooden cross, Jesus gave himself fully for you. When he did that, he didn't make a whole load of excuses – so neither should we! Be reliant on the power of the Holy Spirit – with him, anything is possible! Let him in and then let him go!

Imagine that Jesus is with you and calling you to go with him – as he leaves through the door don't let it be you left behind! Let's pray that churches will be empty because we are willing to give it all up for God!

Let God in and let the Holy Spirit get going! In fact, let's go for it! What's your excuse?

LET US PRAY
And finally...

READING THE SCRIPT

When you are much younger, it becomes very easy to learn something like the Lord's Prayer. It surrounded me back in the eighties when I was a wee lad in just shorts and hand-knitted cardigans. Schools were allowed to use it in assemblies without actually bothering to check for political correctness. Thriving Sunday Schools were teaching it too! The wonder piece from Matthew 6 was always on my mind.

Today, the Lord's Prayer isn't as well taught, and we have several different versions. When you go to church, you're not sure which one you'll be getting. It's always fun to be the only one in a congregation forgiving 'trespasses' when people all around are concentrating on saying 'sins'!

But sins or trespasses don't really matter (in the oral sense, of course!) At the end of the day, God understands your sentiments and exactly what it is you are trying to say. I often feel that we should concentrate on saying a version of the prayer that we have to think about. That way we can really mean what we say and are not reciting lines from memory. The next time you're asked to do the Lord's Prayer – read it from somewhere and find out what it is you're actually praying. It's an incredibly powerful prayer and one with great promises.

As I conclude this book and reflections on a stage in my life, there is one thing that I realise. We always need to keep in close touch with God and to keep praying, whatever the language we use.

After all, prayers like that can help to change the world. Let's do it together!

READING THE SCRIPT

The Traditional View
Our Father who art in heaven
Hallowed be thy name
Thy Kingdom come
Thy will be done
On earth as it is in heaven
Give us this day our daily bread
And forgive us our trespasses
As we forgive those who trespass against us
And lead us not into temptation
But deliver us from evil
For thine is the Kingdom
The power and the glory
For ever and ever
Amen

For those that have swallowed a dictionary
My supreme creator, residing in rapture
Your title may be forever sanctified
May your sovereignty transpire
And may your command be obeyed
Within this globe as it is in paradise
Nourish us with suitable provisions continually
Exonerate our transgressions
As we exonerate any transgressions upon ourselves
Do not lure us into any enticements
But liberate us from iniquity
Possession of the realm is yours
As is the supremacy and the splendour
Ceaselessly
So be it.

For the more casual
Hey there, Dad, listening to me
Your name is going to be forever so, so fantastic!
We want to see you be the boss of the whole world.
And everything you want, we want it to be done
Right here, just like it is done where you are
Feed us, Dad, feed us with what we need to live.
And when we mess up, we're sorry. Let us off.
Just like we let off anyone who messes us around
Don't let things you don't like become so appealing,
In fact, make sure we aren't going towards bad stuff
You are the number one, Dad
You're in control and you're just wonderful
Every day, every week, every year, all the time
Ta ta for now, love me.

OTHER PRODUCTS FROM SIMON COOPER

Simon is an author, preacher and a singer/songwriter with a wide collection of music available to buy.

For more on the CD's, contact Slice Innovations.

CDS

CONVINCED!
My Life's Spread EP

CONVINCED!
Take 72 EP

SIMON COOPER
Experimental EP

THE LENT PROJECT
Echoes of Empty Streets
(In aid of Shelter)

Log onto:
www.sliceinnovations.co.uk/shop
For all your Christian resources and fair trade products

SLICE

Making Dreams Reality

- Complete Event Management from Conception to Evaluation
- In-house Merchandising and Publishing
- Inspirational Retreats, Events & Resources

www.sliceinnovations.co.uk

Find out more about our events and resources.
Slice Innovations is also the home of

Crack pots

156